Sewing Green

25 PROJECTS MADE WITH REPURPOSED & ORGANIC MATERIALS

Plus Tips & Resources for Earth-Friendly Stitching

Betz White

Photographs by John Gruen

STC CRAFT/A MELANIE FALICK BOOK   STEWART, TABORI & CHANG   NEW YORK

Contents

Eco-Logic

Eco-Innovators

As early as six or seven years old, I remember feeling a sense of injustice in the world. How could people litter and pollute? I wondered.

Growing up in southern California in the early 1970s, I was keenly aware of ecological issues. Every day, it seemed, I was exposed to messages from the media, such as Woodsy Owl, who told us, "Give a hoot, don't pollute!" And typical of the Los Angeles area, my elementary school had occasional "smog days" during which we were kept indoors during recess because of the poor air quality. All of this made a lasting impression on me, and as an adult I have always made an effort to tread lightly. In recent years I've even tried to make environmentally friendly choices when I'm engaging in one of my greatest passions—sewing.

Sewing is an ancient and universal craft, a skill once necessary for survival. Although now considered to be more of a creative or leisure activity, sewing remains useful, practical, and, by nature, eco-friendly. As a little girl I played under my mother's sewing table while she made clothes and curtains for our family—partly as a hobby and partly to save money. The youngest of three children, I was no stranger to repurposed clothing, only we called them hand-me-downs. In my teens I discovered thrift shops and began experimenting with refashioning "new" outfits from secondhand clothing. At the time I didn't realize I was being eco-conscious—rather, I was trying to create something unique on a babysitter's budget. But I found that sewing my own belongings, whether altering an existing item or creating something new, taught me to be resourceful and creative. Through the years I continued to sew and eventually earned a degree in fashion design. From the hand-me-downs my mother altered to fit me, to the senior prom dress we refashioned from her 1950s ball gown, to the garments I designed for major apparel manufacturers after finishing college, to the clothes and toys I've sewn for my own kids, sewing has been a cornerstone in my life.

Introduction

So it seems that my early experiences with Woodsy Owl, stitching, and resourcefulness have been brewing in my subconscious all these years as a prelude to writing this book. The idea for *Sewing Green* finally materialized after I finished my first book, *Warm Fuzzies*, which focuses on projects stitched from recycled felted sweaters. While I frequented thrift stores in search of the wool sweaters I needed for *Warm Fuzzies*, naturally I spotted many other second-hand treasures. My mind ran away with me as I faced the reality of excess in our culture and thought of ways to recycle what I was seeing—not just clothing but tablecloths, sheets, placemats, purse handles, belts, and more. I even began to look at non-fabrics, such as Tyvek envelopes and Mylar juice packs, as fair game for sewing. I began to research eco-friendly fabrics made from either recycled materials, such as plastic water bottles, or byproducts of other industries like corn and soy. I read about organically grown cotton and how its pesticide-free cultivation is gentle on the planet. I sought out the stories of clothing designers who incorporate sound environmental choices into their businesses and lifestyles. I found all of this information to be so inspiring that eventually there was no way that I could not write this book.

My hope, as I invite you to explore the pages of *Sewing Green*, is that sewing will become (or will continue to be) a meaningful expression in your life while you simultaneously embrace this earth-friendly approach. This book combines a time-honored tradition with a commitment to protecting the environment. When you make the choice to use sustainable or recycled materials, you'll see just how compatible sewing is with being green. And most importantly, you'll ensure an enduring legacy—both in creating a handmade heirloom as well as sustaining traditions—for generations to come. You may even be inspired to let this environmental mindfulness spill into other areas of your life, from minor changes like bringing your own reusable bags to the grocery store, to bigger ones like riding your bike to work (or maybe the fabric store or library). But for now, keep it simple, start somewhere, and start sewing green.

CHAPTER 1
Thinking Green

GETTING INTO THE
ECO-FRIENDLY MINDSET

Chances are, you're already very much aware of the concept of "living green." The media bombards us with facts and figures about everything from global warming and melting glaciers to buying the right lightbulb in order to offset our carbon footprint. With all of the hype, it's easy to start feeling a little green fatigue.

But this book is not about guilt and sacrifice; it's about creating style with a conscience, and merging our love of craft with our love of the planet. When it comes to sewing, I have found that I am most satisfied with my projects when I use materials that I know won't have a negative impact on the planet—or better yet, may have a positive impact! Two ways I do this are by using repurposed fabrics or fabrics made from organic or sustainable materials.

REPURPOSED SEWING MATERIALS

Rather than making a beeline for the fabric store for new sewing and crafting materials, check out resale shops first for used clothing and linens that you can repurpose to get the fabrics you need. Thrift-store chains are located around the country in big cities as well as small towns. You can find shops in your area by looking in your local telephone directory or by going to thriftyplanet.com (a directory of thrift stores nationwide) or thethriftshopper.com (a national directory of charity-driven thrift stores). For the most part, chain thrift stores are clean, friendly, and well organized, and often have discount days when items are marked down. Flea markets, garage and estate sales, and church rummage sales, are also good resources for unique and inexpensive items. As refashioning and retro styles gain popularity, some consignment shops and resale boutiques mark up certain items and label them "vintage." Rather than looking for vintage items to repurpose in higher-end shops, you might find some great deals at websites like eBay.com and craigslist.com. Even some chain thrift stores such as Goodwill have started selling vintage goods online (shopgoodwill.com).

And finally, be sure to look in your own closet (or the closet of a shopaholic friend who won't mind unloading a few secondhand items). In a culture of "fast fashion," it's far too easy to buy into disposable trends only to cast them aside at season's end. Take another look and try to imagine what last year's must-have could become!

WHAT TO LOOK FOR IN A THRIFT STORE

Resale shops are such a rich and diverse resource for reusable materials that it is sometimes hard to know where to begin and what to look for. The departments you'll want to scope out will vary depending on what repurposing project you have in mind. I like to hit every department just to be sure I don't miss anything, but I'm hard core.

Apparel

Being a big knitwear fan, the sweater rack is always my first stop. Look for non-washable wool and cashmere sweaters, which are great for felting and making into slippers (page 148) or blankets (page 116). Long skirts in heavy-duty denim, corduroy, or suede can yield a fair amount of fabric for reuse in projects such as pillows (page 40) or bags (see the denim shopping bag on page 94). Mens' and womens' wool suit jackets and coats can add a variety of texture and pattern to your fabric stash (try the trivet and coasters on page 20). And a bold vintage dress shirt can liven up a project with retro style, such as a wallet (page 62) or an apron (page 14).

Linens

Here's where you'll be able to find items that are big enough to use as yardage and don't require a lot of deconstructing, such as bedspreads, curtains, and tablecloths. Look for '70s retro-print bedsheets (used for the pants on page 28) and pillowcases (for the skirt on page 124 or the sundress on page 128), tablecloths (see the napkins on page 24 or the wrap skirt on page 80), and placemats (for the beach tote on page 120). If you're lucky, you might even find a crocheted afghan or a vintage chenille bedspread, which can be cut up and made into pillows or bags or reused as accents in a variety of projects.

THRIFT-STORE SHOPPING:
MAJOR SCORES AND MINOR PITFALLS

Once you've hunted and gathered until your cart is
full and your heart's content, go back through it all and give it a
second look. Now is the time to double-check for stains, damages,
and other dilemmas! If possible, take your cart to a window and
inspect everything in good light.

STAINS

There's no guarantee that a stain will come out in the
laundry at home. Think about what you might make out of the item and
decide if there is enough material to work with even if the stain doesn't
come out. If you really love the fabric and it is damaged or stained, consider
if that area can be removed and the rest reserved "for parts."

MOTH HOLES

Often donated wool items are there for a reason. Hold wool sweaters
and suit jackets up to the light to check for moth holes. One or two can most
likely be worked around, but more than that might be problematic.
Bear in mind that if felting is your intention, the holes will not close up
during the felting process.

THAT STINKS

Listen to your nose and abandon all hope for something that
just doesn't smell right. Whether it's mildew or mothballs, it's not
worth trying to salvage.

TALES OF DECONSTRUCTION

Now that you've acquired a fresh stash of secondhand materials,
it's time to get them prepared for their next life.

LAUNDERING

Assuming the care labels are still intact, launder all machine-washable items according to the manufacturer's directions. If you're unsure of the item's fiber content, err on the side of caution. For delicate fabrics like silk and linen, or fragile fabrics such as vintage hand-kerchiefs, hand-wash using a mild detergent and lay flat to dry. For non-machine washable (dry clean only) wool items, don't bother to dry clean—you can simply air them out on a clothesline on a sunny day. You can also give wool items a 15-minute tumble in the dryer on a low to medium heat setting to put an end to any insect issues that may have followed you home. For information about felting wool items, see page 138.

CUTTING

Sharp fabric shears and a seam ripper are all you'll need to deconstruct your garments. If you're using a garment purely for its fabric, you will want to salvage the greatest amount of fabric. Start by trimming away any lining with fabric shears or a seam ripper. If possible, open up the garment's side seams, darts, hems, or anything else that is sewn together, using a seam ripper.

Pull out the remaining threads and press smooth with an iron from the wrong side of the fabric.

Note that if you have a particular project in mind that retains some of the elements of the original garment (such as the apron on page 14, or the denim shopping bag on page 94, follow the deconstruction tips given in the step-by-step directions for that particular project.

KEEPING

Hang on to hardware such as buttons, buckles, D-rings, zippers, and straps, which can all be removed with fabric shears or a seam ripper for future use. It is also possible to gently remove more delicate trims like lace and ribbon with a seam ripper. Use a little liquid seam sealant on the ends of the trims to prevent them from unraveling.

TOSSING

Most lining fabrics will be too worn or flimsy to reuse. Interfacings and other stabilizers should be discarded. Any worn-out areas (think threadbare elbows and frayed sleeve cuffs) are not worth saving. Whether or not you should hang on to shoulder pads is entirely up to you.

Accessories

You'll definitely want to put on your "What else can this be?" thinking cap when visiting the accessory department. This is a great place to find belts or neckties that can be made into handles for a tote bag, or silk scarves that can be reused as gift wrap (see page 65). One of my favorite tips is to check out the purse straps—many bags and purses are unappealing as is, but have great handles that can be easily removed and attached to a handmade bag.

Craft Bin

Fabric remnants, yarn, buttons, trims and other so-called bric-a-brac can be found at bargain prices in the craft supply area. Sometimes these are gathered in clear plastic "grab bags" for less than a buck. Buy one, use what you like, then pass on the leftovers to a crafty friend.

NON-FABRICS: RECYCLING BEYOND THE BLUE BIN

Look no further than your own kitchen, mailbox, or garage to find unique materials with which to sew. This time I'm not referring to pillowcases and tablecloths—I mean packaging. It seems that modern advances in product packaging have yielded a tremendous amount of waste, and even the most conscientious consumers find themselves with undesirable packaging on their hands. For example, nary a kids' soccer game occurs without a post-game drink supplied in an individual Mylar juice pouch. While these are not recyclable, they can be sewn into the auto sunshade on page 110, which puts the reflective quality of the silver Mylar to a good use. Tyvek envelopes (made from high-density polyethylene, HDPE) are a durable and lightweight way to send something through the mail, but when they arrive in your mailbox, hang on to them and create the stylish and practical tote on page 58. Some other stash-worthy non-fabrics for which you might find a fabulous crafty purpose are rice bags, vinyl shower curtains, bubble wrap, plastic tarps, and vinyl banners. Once you start channeling your inner packrat, you'll see ways to transform all sorts of "trash" into useful items! When brainstorming ways that you might use nontraditional materials, it helps to think about the unique properties particular to that material. Is it waterproof? Insulating? Lightweight? Reflective? Consider what kinds of sewn objects could benefit from these properties and let your imagination go wild.

ECO-FRIENDLY NEW SEWING MATERIALS

When you can't find just what you're looking for secondhand, sometimes it makes sense to use new materials. Thankfully, the demand for organic and environmentally sustainable fabric has risen in recent years, and, as a result, producers are becoming more eco-conscious.

Organic fabrics are made from fibers grown or raised according to organic standards, usually meaning without pesticides, herbicides, or synthetic hormones. Fabrics made from other eco-friendly materials, such as cork or recycled polyester, may not be certified organic, but are often naturally sustainable or use recycled materials. New technologies are being developed all the time to make the manufacturing of these fabrics even more benign and eco-friendly.

Choosing eco-friendly fabric is not always a simple task since there are many variables affecting the environmental impact of a particular fiber. Two of the most important variables are cultivation (Where is the fiber grown? Is it local, or

does it travel a great distance to be milled?) and production (What, if any, chemicals are used to process the fiber? Are the dyes low impact or natural?). Our safest approach is to educate ourselves and make decisions based on our areas of concern and best judgment. For the latest information about eco-friendly fabrics, visit Oeko-Tex Standard (oekotex.com), Organic Trade Association (ota.com), and Global Organic Textile Standard (global-standard.org).

Following are descriptions of the most common types of eco-friendly fabrics. (For more information on the specific brands used in this book and to find out where they can be purchased, check the Resources on page 141.)

Organic Cotton

While cotton provides half the world's fiber needs, the cultivation of conventionally grown cotton involves 25 percent of the world's pesticide use, more than any other crop. Organic cotton, on the other hand, is grown without chemicals, using methods that have a low impact on the environment.

Organic Wool

Today's growing expansion of organic agriculture even reaches wool production. To be certified as organic wool, the sheep producing it must be raised on organic feed without the use of synthetic hormones or pesticides or overgrazing of the land. Organic wool fabric is not chemically treated and is naturally breathable, fire retardant, and dust-mite resistant.

Hemp

Hemp is known for its durability as well as its comfort. The more hemp fabric is used, the softer it gets, and it is naturally resistant to the damaging effects of mold and ultraviolet light from the sun. Because it is derived from a plant that grows extremely fast, it produces more fiber yield per acre than any other source and is highly renewable. Hemp is naturally pest resistant and is often grown organically since it grows easily with little to no pesticides.

Bamboo

Because bamboo grows quickly and needs no pesticides or herbicides, bamboo fiber is all natural and easily renewable (though it is not certified organic since there are currently no standards for certification). Bamboo fabric is breathable and moisture wicking, making it cool in the summer and warm in the winter. Its natural antibacterial properties keep it from absorbing and retaining odors.

Cork

Cork fabric, or "cork leather," is a natural product made from the bark of the cork oak tree. It has many unique properties —it is lightweight, waterproof, stain resistant, rot resistant, versatile, soft to the touch, and yet is as durable as leather. Because cork bark can be removed without damaging the tree, it is a renewable resource.

Corn (PLA)

Polylactic acid (PLA) polymer is made from the dextrose extracted from corn. Fabrics made from PLA have the comfort and hand of natural fibers such as cotton and wool, while having the performance, cost, and easy-care characteristics of synthetics. Variations of PLA are also available for use as quilt batting and pillow forms. It is soft, hypoallergenic, breathable, and natural.

Recycled Polyester (PET)

Recycled polyester is a type of fiber that is made from post-consumer polyester (polyethylene terephthalate or PET), such as the material that is used in plastic soda bottles. PET can be recycled into many types of fabrics, such as fleece and canvas, making it a durable and wearable eco-friendly option. It is also used in carpets, home furnishings, auto upholsings, and fiberfill.

CHAPTER 2

Projects

Striped Café Apron

This striped café apron reuses fabrics and details from men's dress shirts, adding an ironic twist to the stereotype that domestic chores are "women's work." Just rearrange the elements—a pocket here or a placket there—and you've got yourself a smart way to protect your clothing from stains. The directions below provide instructions for a tailored apron (with a crisp waistband and pleats, shown on the right on the facing page) and for a gathered apron (with soft shirring and rickrack trim, shown on the left on the facing page).

Materials

1 dress shirt sized L-XXL, with chest pocket, for Tailored Apron. *(For Gathered Apron, if you want to mix patterns, you'll need 2 dress shirts: 1 main shirt, designated in instructions as Shirt A; and second shirt in contrasting fabric, designated as Shirt B.)*

1 yard of ½"-wide rickrack trim *(for Gathered Apron)*

1⅓ yards of ⅝"-wide twill tape or grosgrain ribbon *(for Gathered Apron)*

Thread in a coordinating color

Fabric shears

Seam ripper

DRESS SHIRTS

When choosing a shirt for this project, consider these elements:

○ Many, but not all, dress shirts have chest pockets. A pocket is a great detail to reuse on an apron because it's already sewn, nicely shaped, and handy in the kitchen.

○ Shirts in sizes Large to XX-Large will yield the most fabric. You want at least 16" of length between the bottom of the pocket and the front hem, and at least 24" in width across the chest.

○ Often newer shirts are treated to be wrinkle-free and stain-repellant. Check the label for these qualities when selecting a shirt to convert—these are bonus features for an apron.

○ Some collar stands have labels with phrases like "Wrinkle-Free" or "Pinpoint Oxford" or bearing a brand name. Consider leaving these labels in place on the stand since most can be used as a hanging loop for the apron—and they might also convey a little attitude (like "Classic" or "Slim Cut").

Step 4
Make tucks for Tailored Apron.

¼" - ½" tucks

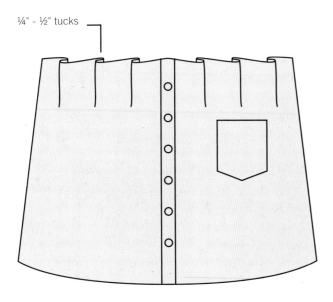

TAILORED APRON

❶ Deconstruct Shirt Details

Using fabric shears, remove the shirt's collar *and* collar stand together (the narrow strip at the neck that supports the collar and houses the shirt's top button and buttonhole) by cutting away the shirt ½" below the stand's bottom edge. Open up the seam at the stand's bottom edge by placing the tip of a seam ripper under the topstitching and gently ripping out the stitches across the stand's entire bottom edge. Remove the ½" strip of material left after cutting the collar away from the body of the shirt. The collar/stand will become the apron's front waistband.

❷ Remove Shirt Pocket

Using fabric shears, cut the front of the shirt along the sides and bottom of the chest pocket as close to the pocket edge as possible but leaving ½" of fabric extending above the pocket's top edge. Do not use the seam ripper to remove the pocket from the shirt fabric. Set the pocket aside.

❸ Prepare Apron Front

You will use the lower front half of the shirt as the apron front. Lay the shirt out flat on a work surface, with the front buttoned and facing up. Starting at the hem, cut up along the side seams. Next cut straight across the chest, perpendicular to the front button placket just below where the pocket was. Measure the length from the hem to the top cut edge, which will be the length of your apron, or about 16", depending on the shirt you are using. If you want to shorten the apron, trim off any excess along the upper raw edge, but do not trim off the shirttail, which will become the apron's hem.

With the shirt still buttoned, pin the front button-placket edges together, and topstitch the placket's left side, following the original stitching line. Then topstitch down the placket's right side, again following the original stitching line. Hem the apron's sides by double-turning and pressing each cut side edge ⅛" to the wrong side, and then edge-stitching (see page 133) the double-folded edge.

❹ Tucks and Such

Lay the collar/stand (which will become the front waistband) on your work surface with the back of the collar/stand facing up (the neck button should be on your right and the buttonhole on your left). Lay the apron front flat, right side up, below the collar/stand. The width of the apron front should be about

25-50% wider than the collar/stand. (The Tailored Apron shown at right on page 15 measures 19" wide for the collar/stand and 24" for the full width of the front.)

You will be making several tucks along the top edge of the apron front. Starting about 2" to the right of the placket, fold ¼"-½" of fabric into a tuck folded to the right, and pin the tuck in place. *Note: If you are using a striped shirt, the easiest way to establish the tucks is to simply follow the stripes. Make a vertical fold along one stripe, and place it on top of another stripe to the right, creating a small tuck.* Measure about 2" to the right of the first tuck (or measure by counting the number of stripes), and pin another tuck into place. After making three tucks on the right, repeat this process on the left side of the placket, folding the tucks to the left (see the drawing at left). Stop to compare the width of the collar/stand with your tucked apron front, which should be about the same width or slightly smaller than the collar/stand. If the apron front is still wider than the collar/stand, add another tuck on the right and left of the placket or adjust the depth of the existing tucks.

❺ Attach Front Waistband

With the collar/stand still positioned above the apron front and both still right side up, open the bottom edge of the stand, and insert the apron front's top edge. An even ¼"of the apron front's tucked top edge should be sandwiched between the stand's two layers. Re-pin through all layers, maintaining the placement of the tucks. Edge-stitch across the bottom edge of the stand, securing all layers. *Note: Some shirts have what's called a "locker loop" inserted at the center-back yoke, which is a great detail to reuse. If your shirt has a locker loop, remove it with a seam ripper. Then, when sandwiching the apron front into the collar stand, insert and pin the ends of the locker loop at the center front on top of the button placket. The ends will be secured when you edge-stitch the edge of the waistband. Now you'll have a loop to use to hang up your apron!*

❻ Attach Pocket

Fold and press the top-edge extension on the pocket you cut out in Step 2 towards the back of the pocket, leaving ¹⁄₁₆" showing from the front. Lay the pocket on the apron front, about 2½" to the right of the placket and 4" below the waistband. *Note: If your fabric is striped, use the stripes as a guide to align the pocket edges.*

Step 6
Attach pocket.

½" fabric extension

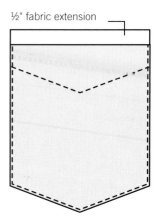

½" fabric extension folded down leaving ¹⁄₁₆" above pocket

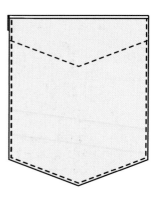

¹⁄₁₆" folded extension and sides of pocket topstitched

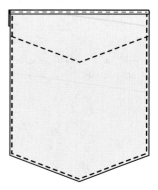

Pin the pocket into place, and topstitch it to the apron, following the existing stitching on the pocket's sides and bottom. Then stitch across the top ¹⁄₁₆" folded edge of the shirting showing behind the pocket itself (see the drawings at left), taking care not to stitch the pocket shut!

❼ Make Apron Ties
Cut two 2½" x 24" strips of fabric from the remaining shirt sleeves. Fold one strip in half lengthwise, with right sides together, and stitch a ¼" seam across one end and down the length of the raw edges, creating a long tube. Use a chopstick to push the sewn end of the tube—and the tube itself—right side out. Press the turned tube flat. Fold in the tube/tie's raw edges ½" to the wrong side, and pin the tie to the back of the waistband, overlapping the waistband by 1". Attach the end of the waistband tie by topstitching a box over the end with an X inside the box. Repeat this process for the second tie.

GATHERED APRON

❶ Deconstruct Shirt Details
Starting with Shirt A, remove the collar from the collar stand by cutting the collar off as close to the stand's top edge as possible. (Be precise because this will be the top edge of the apron's waistband. You may need to pick out any stray threads that remain on the stand's edge.) Begin removing the collar stand from the shirt by cutting away the shirt ½" below the bottom edge of the stand. Open up the seam at the stand's bottom edge by placing the tip of a seam ripper underneath the topstitching. Gently rip open the seam across the entire edge, and remove the ½" strip of material left from cutting away the body of the shirt. Discard the collar and the ½" strip. The stand will become the apron's front waistband.

❷ Remove Shirt Pocket
Follow the directions for Step 2 for the Tailored Apron to cut the pocket from Shirt A.

❸ Prepare Apron Front
You will use the lower back portion of Shirt B as the apron front. Lay the shirt out flat on a work surface, facing down. Starting at the hem, cut up the side seams. Next cut straight across the back, perpendicular to the side seams at the widest part of the shirt. Measure the length from the hem to the top cut edge, which will be the length of your apron, or about 16", depending on the shirt you are using. If you want to shorten the apron, trim off any excess along the upper raw edge, but do not trim off the shirttail, which will become the apron's hem.

Hem the apron's sides by double-turning each cut side edge ⅛" to the wrong side, and edge-stitching the double-folded edge. Add rickrack trim along the existing hem by pinning it along the hem's wrong side, with the rickrack points sticking out from the hem. Topstitch the rickrack in place.

❹ Gathers and Such

Lay the collar stand (which will become the front waistband) on your work surface with the inside of the stand facing up (the neck button should be on your left and the buttonhole on your right). Lay the apron front flat, right side up, below the collar/stand. The apron front should be about 25-50% wider than the collar/stand. (In the Gathered Apron shown at left on page 15, the stand measures 18" and the full apron front 25".)

You will be making gathers along the apron front's top edge before attaching it to the front waistband/collar stand. To create gathers, use the longest stitch length possible on your sewing machine to sew two parallel rows of straight stitches ¼" from the top edge of the apron front and ⅛" apart. Do not trim the thread tails.

Grab the tails of the two top threads running along the right edge of the fabric, and gently pull them from one end to create gathers in the fabric. Repeat the process from the fabric's left edge, and distribute the gathers evenly across the top of the apron front. Stop to compare the width of the apron front with that of the waistband. Adjust the gathers as needed so the apron front and waistband are more or less the same width.

❺ Attach Front Waistband

With the collar stand positioned above the apron front, open the bottom edge of the stand and insert the top edge of the apron front. An even ¼" of the apron front's top edge should be sandwiched between the two layers of the stand. Pin through all layers, maintaining an even distribution of gathers. Topstitch across the bottom edge of the stand, securing all layers.

❻ Attach Pocket

Fold and press the top-edge extension on the pocket you cut out in Step 2 towards the back of the pocket, leaving ¹⁄₁₆" showing from the front. Lay the pocket on the apron front, about 2½" to the right of center, and 4" below the waistband. *Note: If your fabric is striped, use the stripes as a guide to align the pocket edges.*

Before pinning the pocket in place, slip a length of rickrack between the pocket and apron front, following the pocket's side and bottom edges and folding under the rickrack's raw ends for a clean finish. Pin and topstitch the rickrack and pocket to the apron, following the existing stitching on the pocket's sides and bottom edge. Then stitch across the top ¹⁄₁₆" folded edge of the shirting showing behind the pocket itself (see the drawings on the facing page), taking care not to stitch the pocket shut!

❼ Make Apron Ties

Attach two 24" lengths of ⅝"-wide twill tape or ribbon to each end of the waistband: After folding one end of one tie ½" to the wrong side, pin that end to one end of the back of the waistband, overlapping the edges by 1". Attach the end of the tie and waistband by topstitching a box over the end with an X inside. Cut the other end of the tie at a 45-degree angle to finish it. Repeat this process for the second tie.

❽ Wear with Abandon!

Whether you're baking cookies with the kids or throwing dinner together after a day at the office, you'll appreciate having a few of these aprons handy.

Penny-Rug Trivet and Coasters

This trivet-and-coaster set is a perfect example of old-fashioned craft meets contemporary style—clean, graphic shapes are cut from reclaimed wool scraps and accented with hand-stitched details. Each design can be made individually to create a set of coasters (great as a gift!) or sewn together to create a trivet. Appliquéd layers make a thick base just right for insulating a hot dish or absorbing moisture from a cold drink.

Materials

Assorted wool scraps *(any densely woven or felted wool fabric is suitable, such as wool felt, melton wool, or wool suiting)* totaling approximately ¼ yard

Lightweight yarn or embroidery floss in coordinating colors, a few yards of each

Thread matching wool scraps

Double-sided fusible webbing, two 8½" x 11" sheets

Fabric shears

Paper scissors

Tapestry needle with sharp point

Pencil

SOURCING WOOL

There are lots of options when it comes to finding wool materials to repurpose for this project. Visit thrift stores or flea markets to find melton wool coats, long skirts or pants made of wool suiting, or wool flannel shirts. Felted wool from sweaters (see Step 1 on page 23) works nicely for the backing of the trivet and coasters.

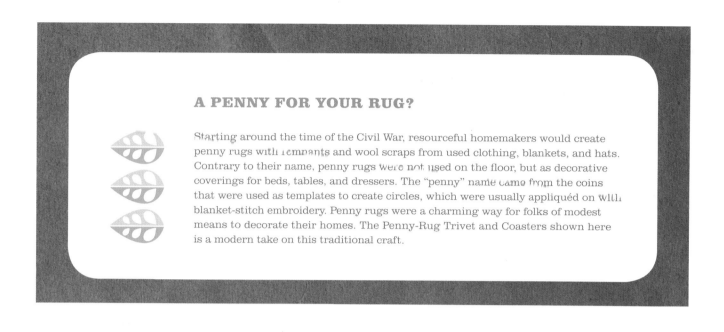

A PENNY FOR YOUR RUG?

Starting around the time of the Civil War, resourceful homemakers would create penny rugs with remnants and wool scraps from used clothing, blankets, and hats. Contrary to their name, penny rugs were not used on the floor, but as decorative coverings for beds, tables, and dressers. The "penny" name came from the coins that were used as templates to create circles, which were usually appliquéd on with blanket-stitch embroidery. Penny rugs were a charming way for folks of modest means to decorate their homes. The Penny-Rug Trivet and Coasters shown here is a modern take on this traditional craft.

TRIVET AND COASTER PATTERNS

(Photocopy at 200%)

For each coaster, cut:
1 background square
1 backing liner square
1 of each appliqué being used

For trivet, cut:
4 background squares
1 of each appliqué being used
8"-square backing liner

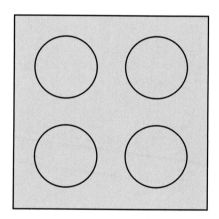

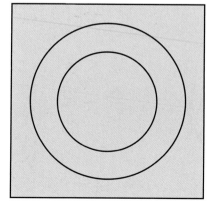

❶ Prepare Fabrics

Start by deconstructing the garments you've selected, reclaiming the largest amount of fabric possible. Using fabric shears, cut apart the major seams. Remove and discard (or save for another project) linings, trims, and bulky understructures, such as interfacings and shoulder pads. Launder the fabrics with detergent in the washing machine on hot to "full," or felt, the wool, allowing it to shrink and become soft and dense. Dry the fabric in the dryer on low. If needed, steam the fabric flat on the wrong side with an iron on the wool setting. (See also page 138 for more information on felting wool.)

❷ Cut Background Pieces

FOR 4 COASTERS

Using fabric shears, cut four 4" squares of wool in your desired background colors and four 4" squares of wool for a backing liner.

FOR TRIVET

Using fabric shears, cut four 4" squares of wool in your desired background colors and one 8" square of wool for a backing liner.

❸ Create Appliqué Shapes

Photocopy the patterns at left, enlarging them as indicated. Using a pencil and the patterns, trace the appliqué shapes you want to use onto the paper side of a piece of fusible webbing. With paper scissors, cut out the shapes just outside the pencil lines, not on these lines. Following the manufacturer's directions, fuse the webbing to the wrong side of the appliqué fabric with an iron. Cut out the fused fabric shapes along the pencil lines.

❹ Make Coasters

Peel off the paper backing from the webbing on the appliqué shapes, and layer the shapes, webbing side down, onto the right side of the corresponding background squares. Cover the work with a press cloth, and fuse the shapes to the background squares with a steam iron.

Using a tapestry needle and yarn or floss in a color coordinating with the background layer on which you're stitching the appliqué (for example, for stitching a pink circle on top of brown, use brown yarn/floss), blanket-stitch (see page 135) around each appliqué design.

Apply fusible webbing to each 4" backing square. Then peel away the paper from the webbing, and fuse the backing liner to the back of the appliquéd square, using a press cloth to cover the work. For a crisp finish, edge-stitch (see page 133) around the coaster's edges.

❺ Make Trivet

Follow the coaster instructions in Steps 3 and 4 (omitting the last paragraph of Step 4) to create four different appliqué designs. Then, instead of sewing a 4"-square backing to each design, back the whole trivet with an 8" square of wool: Apply fusible webbing to the wrong side of the 8"-square backing liner, and remove the paper backing from the webbing. Then lay the 8" square with the webbing side up, and place the four 4"-square designs on top of the webbing, right side up and aligning the corners of the four designs in the center. Cover the work with a press cloth, and fuse together the trivet and backing liner. To help secure the backing and finish the edges nicely, edge-stitch each square along its four edges.

❻ Put Kettle On

Brew yourself a pot of tea or coffee…and try out your new trivet and coasters while you're at it.

Vintage Napkins and Trim Napkin Rings

When crafting with vintage textiles and trimmings, even leftover scraps may be too precious to throw away. Draw from your stash of remnants and trims to create an assortment of unique napkins and napkin rings. Tablecloths, aprons, and tea towels that have seen better days can also be repurposed into napkins. Sew a whole batch for your household, and make paper napkins obsolete.

Materials

Napkins
(For one napkin)
16" square of medium-weight woven fabric, such as linen, cotton calico, or broadcloth
2 yards of trim, such as rickrack, bias tape, or ribbon
Coordinating thread
Fabric shears

Napkin Rings
(For one ring)
2 plastic rings (about 1¾" in diameter), produced by breaking open sealed cap on large plastic milk or juice container
At least 1 yard of ¼" to ½" trim, such as rickrack, bias tape, or ribbon; additional 1 to 1½ yards of ½"-wide rickrack trim for optional embellishment
Assortment of vintage or other buttons (optional)
Thread matching trim
Hand-sewing needle
Hot glue gun

BOTTLE CAPS AND RINGS

Although a plastic bottle can be recycled, its cap and ring (the piece left at the container's neck when you break open the sealed cap) oftentimes cannot be. Now you can use the rings to create these napkin rings. To remove the ring on a plastic bottle, use a small screwdriver to gently pry the ring up and over the ridges at the bottle's neck. Be careful, though, since too much force can stretch or break the ring.

❶ Make and Trim Napkin

Cut a 16" square from your fabric. If you're using vintage fabrics, be sure to avoid any holes, flaws, or noticeable fading when cutting out the napkin. The trim you're using determines how you'll construct the napkin: Trimming with rickrack or ribbon requires finishing the napkin's edge before applying the trim. Trimming with a bias binding calls for finishing the raw edge with the bias binding itself.

TO TRIM NAPKIN WITH RICKRACK

Lay the fabric wrong side up, and fold and press each edge ⅛" to the wrong side; then edge-stitch (see page 133) the folded edge. Next fold, press, and pin the edges another ⅛" to the wrong side. Align and pin the rickrack along the wrong side of the hem, so the rickrack's points extend past the napkin's folded edges. Slightly overlap the beginning and ending edges of the rickrack, and cut off any excess. Working on the napkin's wrong side, straight-stitch the trim to the napkin, stitching along the center of the rickrack and pivoting (see page 140) at the corners, and backstitching (see page 133) at the beginning and end of your stitching. (Because rickrack zigzags back and forth, it turns corners easily without needing to be mitered like ribbon or bias binding at corners.)

TO TRIM NAPKIN WITH BIAS BINDING

Start by laying the fabric with the right side up. Then follow the directions on page 136 to bind an edge with bias binding and create mitered corners with the binding.

❷ Make Napkin Ring Base

Using a hot glue gun, glue the two plastic bottle rings together, one on top of the other. Glue one end of the trim inside the joined rings. Passing the trim through the center, wind the trim around the ring, slightly overlapping the previous wrap. Apply a dot of glue inside the ring every few wraps to secure the trim. Keep winding and gluing the trim until the entire ring is covered. Cut the trim's raw end so that it will end on the inside of the ring, and glue the end in place.

> **"It was not until we saw the picture of the earth, from the moon, that we realized how small and how helpless this planet is – something that we must hold in our arms and care for."**
> MARGARET MEAD

❸ Embellish Wrapped Ring (optional)

If you want, you can embellish your wrapped napkin ring with buttons or rickrack flowers (see photo at left). Below are some ideas for adding these trims.

BUTTONS

Choose an assortment of buttons with a common color, shape, or size. With a hand-sewing needle and thread, sew each button to the wrapped ring. For extra stability, add a dot of hot glue beneath the button's edge after you've sewn it in place. And for added dimension, consider gluing one or more small buttons on top of larger ones sewn in place.

RICKRACK FLOWER

Cut two 18"-20" strands of ½"-wide rickrack in two colors. With the cut ends of the rickrack strands aligned, hold the strands one on top of the other, and tack the ends together with a hand-sewing needle and thread. Then slowly crisscross the two strands back and forth, passing one over the other so that the two strands interlock at the rickrack's points. Once the entire length of the strands is interlocked, tack the remaining ends together with the needle and thread.

Next, begin rolling the interlocked rickrack, starting from one end, to form the center of the flower. Once you've got a couple inches rolled, hand-stitch through the base of the roll to anchor it. Then continue rolling the rickrack around the base, stitching along the lower edge of the interlocked rickrack and shaping the upper edges into a flower. Tie off the thread when the flower has reached the desired size. Sew a button in the center of the flower, and attach the completed flower to the ring with hot glue.

RICKRACK ROSEBUDS

Cut one 10" length of ½"-wide rickrack. Fold the length in half, and slowly crisscross the two tails back and forth, passing one over the other so that the two tails interlock at the rickrack's points. Starting with the cut ends, tightly roll the interlocked braid into a bud, and secure it with a pin or two stabbed through the center of the roll. With a hand-sewing needle and thread, stitch through the bottom of the bud several times, catching the points of each layer of rickrack. Tie off and cut the thread. Gently peel back the "petals" from the top of the bud, as desired.

Make two more buds, and attach them to the ring with hot glue. For "leaves," fold two 1" lengths of ¼"-wide ribbon in half, and glue the ends flush to the bottom edges of the outermost rosebuds.

Take-It-Easy Lounge Pants

Everyone needs a little down time. When you do get a chance to kick back, make the most of it with a leisurely pair of lounge pants. They're more stylish than sweats (think comfy, not schlumpy) and simple to make. Try using one or more favorite sheets, like the pair of vintage '70s florals used here, or another soft fabric with a print that suits your personality.

Finished Measurements

Note: The waist measurements are approximate since the waist is elastic.

Small: Waist, 27"; hip, 42"; inseam, 29"
Medium: Waist, 29½"; hip, 44½"; inseam, 29"
Large: Waist, 32½"; hip, 47½"; inseam, 29"

Materials

1 twin-size (or larger) bed sheet, or 2 yards of 60"-wide, lightweight woven fabric, such as cotton calico, broadcloth, or flannel
¼ yard of 45"-wide, contrast-print fabric (optional)
1 yard of 1"-wide waistband elastic
Fabric shears
Paper scissors
Parchment or shelf paper, one 15"-wide roll
Pencil
Large safety pin

❶ Prepare Materials

Prewash and -dry all the fabrics. Using the pattern provided on the pullout sheet at the back of the book, select the size you want to make, place a large piece of white shelf paper over the pattern, and trace the pattern (this allows you to keep the original pattern intact). Use paper scissors to cut out the traced pattern pieces.

❷ Cut Out Front, Back, and Cuffs

If you are using a printed fabric, look at the print's design before you cut the pattern out of the fabric. Some prints have a two-way layout, meaning that the design reads correctly with either end up. Other prints, such as a scenic design or a border print, may work in only one direction. You'll want to be sure that the pattern runs in the same, correct direction for both the front and back of the pants.

Lay out the main fabric on a large work surface. Fold the fabric selvedge to selvedge (or if you are using a sheet, fold it lengthwise, matching the side edges), with the fabric's wrong sides facing together. Lay out the pattern piece for the front and back so that the length of the piece and the marked grain line (see page 139) run parallel to the fold. Secure the pattern pieces by pinning through both layers of fabric. With fabric shears, cut along the edge of the pattern piece through both layers. You will end up with two fronts and two backs, with one set of front and back pieces reversed. Cut out two cuffs, using either the main fabric or the optional contrast fabric.

❸ Sew Legs

Match one front pant piece and one back pant piece, with right sides together. Pin the two pieces along the inseam and the outer side seam. Sew the inseam and the side seam using a straight stitch and a ¼" seam. Finish the seam allowances by zigzag-stitching the raw edges together, and press them to one side (see page 140). Repeat the process for the second leg.

❹ Sew Rise

Turn one pant leg right side out. Slide this right-side-out pant leg inside the pant leg that's still wrong side out, so the right sides of the two legs face together. Match up the inseams and side seams of the two legs, and pin the two along the rise, or crotch area. Sew the rise seam using a straight stitch and a ¼" seam. Finish the seam allowances by zigzag-stitching the raw edges together, and press them to one side. Turn the pants wrong side out; and, working from the wrong side, topstitch the seam allowances to one side 1/16" from the rise seam line. Topstitch a second row 1/8" away from the first, securing the allowances. These two rows of topstitching are critical for maximum comfort.

❺ Sew Cuffs

Fold the cut fabric piece for one cuff end to end, with right sides together. Seam the ends of the cuff with a ¼" seam. Repeat the process for the second cuff, and turn both cuffs right side out.

Place one cuff, right side out, inside the bottom opening of one pant leg, also right side out. Align the cuff seam with the pant leg inseam (the cuff's right side will face the wrong side of the pant leg), and pin and stitch the edges together with a ¼" seam. Pull the cuff out of the pant leg, and press the seam allowances down toward the cuff.

Fold and press the cuff's unsewn edge ¼" to the wrong side. Then bring this folded edge up, so it just covers the seam line attaching the cuff to the pant leg, concealing the seam allowances. Pin the folded cuff into place, evenly distributing the cuff fabric around the opening of the pant leg. Topstitch the cuff in place 1/8" from the fold covering the seam allowances, working from the right side of the leg. Repeat the process for the other cuff.

❻ Make Waistline Casing

Finish the top edge of the pants at the waistline by zigzag-stitching or serging this edge. With the pants turned wrong side out, fold and pin the finished top edge 1½" to the wrong side, creating the waistline casing on the wrong side (inside) of the pants. Starting at the center back, topstitch around the waistline casing 1¼" from the folded edge, leaving a 2" opening at the center back. Loosely measure your waist with a piece of elastic, add 2" to this measurement, and cut the elastic to this measurement. Using a safety pin secured to one end of the elastic, thread the elastic through the casing, taking care not to twist the elastic. Bring the elastic's end out through the back opening, and secure both elastic ends together with the safety pin.

❼ Comfort Check

Almost done! Try on your pants and adjust the elastic at the back opening for comfort, tightening or loosening the elastic as needed and securing the adjusted elastic ends with the safety pin. Zigzag-stitch the elastic ends together at your desired circumference, remove the safety pin, and trim the excess elastic.

Close the casing's opening by topstitching the unsewn section of the first row of stitching. Add another row of topstitching 1/8" below the first to further secure the casing.

❽ Kick Back

Relax and enjoy the sensation of lazing in bed—even if you're not! And since these pants can be made up in a jiffy, why not make another pair as a gift? If you started with a king- or queen-size sheet, you've got fabric to spare.

SEWING LOUNGES

Sewing lounges are cropping up all over in response to the renewed interest in stitching these days. Much like an Internet café, a sewing lounge is a place where DIYers can rent sewing machines by the hour and have access to irons, sergers, cutting tables, and dress forms—perfect for anyone who doesn't have space in her own home for a sewing area, isn't sure she's ready to buy her own equipment, or doesn't feel the need to own her own equipment. While some sewing lounges are extensions of established fabric and quilt stores, others are dedicated sewing spaces where customers can find guidance and a full range of classes, such as garment refashioning and high-end couture techniques. And like sewing circles of yesteryear, a sewing lounge is also a great place to share inspiration and tips, get advice from experts, and make new friends.

Here are a few of the many sewing lounges in the United States. To find sewing lounges in other areas, try entering "sewing lounge" or "stitch lounge" and your city of choice in your favorite Internet search engine.

Bobbin's Nest Studio (Santa Clara, CA)
www.bobbinsnest.com

Etsy Labs (Brooklyn, NY)
www.etsylabs.blogspot.com

First Samples (Austin, TX)
www.firstsamples.com

Kitty Kitty Boom Boom (Durango, CO)
www.kittykittyboomboom.com

Philadelphia Sewing Collective
(Philadelphia, PA) www.phillysewing.org

Quiltology (Chicago, IL)
www.quiltology.com

Sew LA (Los Angeles, CA)
www.sew-la.com

Sewing Lounge (St. Paul, MN)
www.sewinglounge.com

Spark Craft Studios (Cambridge, MA)
www.sparkcrafts.com

Stitch Cleveland (Cleveland, OH)
www.stitchcleveland.com

Stitch Lounge (San Francisco, CA)
www.stitchlounge.com

Stitches (Seattle, WA)
www.stitchesseattle.com

swap-
o-rama-
rama

Wendy Tremayne's credo is that today's "maker" (a person who makes his or her belongings rather than buys them) is the modern revolutionary. In this spirit, Wendy is the founder and producer of the clothing swap and DIY workshops Swap-O-Rama-Rama, hands-on recycling and creativity events that are held in communities all over the world.

A Swap-O-Rama-Rama works something like this: Participants come to the event, usually held in a community space, with a bag of clothes to share. Volunteers sort the garments by category, then participants get to "shop" in a room full of free clothing, finding new treasure from other's so-called trash. To add a dimension of creativity to the swap, local craftspeople set up stations where they offer participants help in everything from mending to silk-screening as they transform their finds. The newly repurposed clothes are tagged with "Modified by Me" labels, and there's even a fashion show at the end to celebrate everyone's creativity.

The spirit of a Swap-O-Rama-Rama is that of a crafty social affair. Mirrors are intentionally absent; people instead rely on each other for help and opinions. "How do I look?" becomes an icebreaker, and soon the event becomes a shared creative experience. The process of altering a garment seems to alter the maker as well. "Once people have the experience of making their own clothes, it changes how they look at the wider world," Wendy says. "I've seen people become transformed. People run out practically screaming about all the things they want to do. You see the spark."

It's a belief in this creative energy—and the freedom it gives people from money and consumption—that led Wendy to create SORR. "To understand consumerism and value, I decided to live for one year on barter, no money," she says. "For each area of my life, I had to be very creative about how I would get what I needed." As a musician, she played gigs at venues that served food. She worked out an arrangement with her roommates to make things for them rather than contribute money toward rent. "For clothing, I chose to create a clothing swap," she says. "After producing a few swaps in my apartment, it seemed clear that there was an impulse for people to be more creative." This focus on not only reusing clothing, but transforming it into an expression of one's own style, is apparent at every SORR.

Wendy, who has a lot of experience organizing events from fundraisers to live performances, produced the first public Swap-O-Rama-Rama in San Francisco in 2005. It drew 500 attendees—many more than anticipated. "There is no creativity in consumerism," Wendy says when contemplating the overwhelming response. "One hundred years ago, all of the items in our lives were made by us or someone we knew. The objects were all imbued with meaning. It wasn't just something that came off a factory assembly line, it was a story about a person and a life." She feels that in today's consumer climate, people's means of expression has been reduced to simply choosing from what is available in stores. "Makers don't make good consumers," she says. "The more you know, the more you can make, the less you're going to buy."

Since its introduction into the world, the Swap-O-Rama-Rama has grown to include more than a few dozen American cities as well as cities in several other countries (including Canada, England, Israel, Turkey, and Panama), and it continues to grow. Each event draws hundreds of people, and an estimated 5,000 to 7,000 pounds of clothing are recycled at each event as a result. While Wendy still organizes some SORRs, local organizers are more often in charge of planning and executing their own. Wendy then offers them everything she can in support: sewing machines (loaned by Janome), a swap planner e-mail list (so that organizers can share information and tips), a page on the Swap-O-Rama-Rama website specifically devoted to each event, and training on how to produce the events efficiently and effectively.

Ultimately, a garment created at a Swap-O-Rama-Rama has staying power. As Wendy notes, "No one's kicking to the curb that garment that they spent the whole day having the greatest time making. That's not going in the trash, that's hanging around for a good long time."

To take part, or for more information on starting a SORR in your hometown, visit swaporamarama.org.

Cashmere Lap Throw— Luxe Redux

Cashmere sweaters are thrift-store gold. When you find them, grab them. Because cashmere is incredibly soft, warm, and lightweight, it's perfect for any type of blanket. This lap throw combines four to five sweaters in compatible colors. The patchwork front is accented by simple appliqués and backed with plush organic cotton velour. And because all the materials are laundered and preshrunk beforehand, the result is both gorgeous and machine-washable. Who knew recycling could be so luxurious?

Finished Measurements
Approximately 45" wide x 60" long

Materials
4 or 5 100% cashmere sweaters, women's or men's
  (Note: Pullovers are preferable to cardigans
  since they yield larger pieces of fabric.)
2 yards of 51"-wide organic cotton velour
Double-sided fusible webbing,
  one 8½" x 11" sheet
Matching thread
Fabric shears
Rotary cutter and cutting mat
Metal-edge ruler
Hand-sewing needle

IN SEARCH OF CASHMERE

When looking for cashmere sweaters in a thrift store, always check more than the sweater racks. Because these sweaters are commonly knitted at a very fine gauge, they are often hung with the blouses and T-shirts. And don't forget to look in the men's department since larger sweaters yield larger pieces of fabric.

Before you buy a sweater, hold it up to the light to check for moth holes. If it has moth holes, look at where they are positioned to see if there is enough good fabric to work with around them. Once you get the sweater home, wash and dry it right away to eliminate the risk of unwanted moths in your house.

QUILTERS—
THE ORIGINAL
REPURPOSERS

Today green-minded sewers often reuse fabrics for clothing and quilts because it helps keep textiles out of our landfills. But throughout history— especially from the post-Civil War era to the Great Depression—materials were scarce and many quilts had to be made from leftover fabric scraps and from what we might call "trash" today. When clothing was no longer wearable, it was deconstructed, and the usable fabric was stitched together to make quilt tops. If batting was not available, blankets, worn-out quilts, and in especially dire times, even newspapers were inserted between the quilt front and back to add warmth. Since new fabrics were often hard to come by, on-hand materials, such as feedsacks, made their way into pieced quilt tops. On occasion even the silk cigar ribbons and colorful textile inserts from tobacco packaging were stitched into unique and complex quilt designs, further demonstrating the quiltmaker's imagination and resourcefulness.

❶ Prepare Materials

Machine-launder the sweaters (washing like colors together) with detergent in hot water, and machine-dry them on a low setting. This will shrink the sweaters slightly and make them softer and fluffier. Machine-wash the velour separately in warm water, and machine-dry it on medium heat.

❷ Deconstruct Sweaters

Using fabric shears, deconstruct the sweaters following the directions on page 8. Lay the four pieces each sweater yields flat. If the pieces are wrinkled, press them with a steam iron on the wool setting, using a press cloth if you're pressing on the fabric's right side (or pressing without one on the back of the fabric).

Using a rotary cutter, cutting mat, and metal-edge ruler, cut the sweater pieces into the largest rectangles possible, maintaining a consistent width. In the blanket shown at right, I used rectangles that were all 15" wide but varied in length. Use the sweater fronts and backs for tall rectangles and the sleeves for shorter ones. Do your best to use all the cashmere—and remember to save your scraps!

❸ Arrange Layout

On a large surface, such as a table, floor, or bed, arrange the rectangles, right side up, in three columns of equal length, adding or taking away rectangles, moving them around, or trimming them down as necessary to get the desired column length and design. Make sure as you work that the right side of the rectangles (originally the outside of the garment) always faces up. To record your layout (so you won't forget it while constructing the throw, which is easy to do), take a digital photo of it, or write numbers on pieces of masking tape to adhere to each corresponding piece of fabric.

❹ Assemble Patchwork Front

Start assembling the patchwork at the bottom of the first column: Flip the bottom rectangle up, so it's right side down on top of the rectangle above it. The rectangles will be right sides together with what are now their bottom edges aligned. Then pin the bottom edges together, and machine-stitch a ¼" seam along them, taking care not to stretch the fabric as you sew and cause the seams to ripple. After joining the first two rectangles, flip the upper rectangle of the joined pair, right side down, on top of the rectangle above it, again aligning, pinning, and sewing their bottom edges together. Repeat this process until you've sewn all the rectangles in the first column; then repeat the process to sew the other two columns of rectangles.

Next, sew the three columns together along their long edges: Begin by lightly steam-pressing each column's seams open from the wrong side. Then lay the first column, right side down, on top of the second column, matching the edges. Pin

and straight-stitch the long edges on the left side together with a ¼" seam. Repeat the process, sewing the third column to the second. Use the metal-edge ruler to square up the blanket by trimming off any uneven edges that may have been produced during sewing. At this point you may be tempted to just stop sewing and curl up in the cashmere softness with a good book, but forge on! It gets even better, I promise.

❺ Make and Attach Backing

Lay out the 2 yards of prewashed velour, right side up. Place the patchwork front on top of the velour, right side down, smoothing out the fabric over the velour and taking care not to stretch it out of shape. Trim the edges of the velour to make it the same size as the patchwork front. With right sides of the patchwork front and backing facing together, pin the patchwork front to the backing around the perimeter of the throw.

Machine-stitch the front to the back with a ¼" seam, leaving a 10" opening on one side for turning the throw right side out. Trim the seam allowances diagonally at the corners to eliminate bulk, and turn the throw right side out. Fold the seam allowances at the opening to the inside, and pin the opening closed. Lightly steam-press the opening on the velour side, being careful to hold the iron just above the velour, so it won't crush the fabric's nap. Using a hand-sewing needle and matching thread, whipstitch (see page 135) the opening closed. Topstitch ¼" from the edge around entire the throw, taking care not to stretch the fabric as you sew.

❻ Apply Appliqués

Cut a 2" strip of fusible webbing for each of the appliqués you want to add to the patchwork (I used five 2" x 4" strips and five 2" x 8" strips), and use an iron to fuse the strips to the back of the remaining sweater-scrap rectangles. Arrange the rectangles on the patchwork front to determine their placement. Then remove the webbing's paper backing, and fuse each rectangle to the patchwork front, covering the rectangle with a press cloth when you fuse it. Pin the areas around each appliqué through both layers to keep the front and back from shifting while you sew the appliqués in place. Then edge-stitch (see page 133) around each appliqué through all layers of the blanket to secure the front to the back.

❼ Time Out

Reward your efforts! Now that you're finished, snuggle up and take a break.

alabama
chanin

All of Alabama Chanin's
products—from clothing
to jewelry to home furnishings — are made in the
most socially and environmentally responsible ways
possible, using recycled or
organic materials and the
talents of local craftspeople.
Most impressively, they
are all made by hand.

Natalie Chanin, founder of Alabama Chanin, was born and raised in Florence, Alabama—an area steeped in the traditions of old-time quilt circles. An innate love of and appreciation for handmade things, combined with a keen concern for sustainability, brought her back to her hometown after twenty-two years away to start her own company.

Through Alabama Chanin, Natalie enlists local seamstresses to create unique pieces of clothing with amazing detail equivalent to that of a lovingly handmade quilt. "Around here, quilting and textiles have long been part of our history," she explains. "So instead of sourcing our manufacturing far away, we have chosen to utilize the skills and knowledge of local artisans, who hand-make every item." These things are made by hand not out of disdain for technology, but rather a desire to preserve these living arts. "Sustainable traditions are a very important part of what we do," says Natalie. "There is something so beautiful about making something with a needle and thread."

In 1978, Natalie left Florence to study design fundamentals at North Carolina State University, which interwove the study of craft and fine art and offered her an intensive, hands-on study of textiles. After working in design and film in New York and Vienna, she returned to Florence in 2000 to make a documentary film called *Stitch,* which she describes as a story of rural America told by those who make and use quilts. She was also looking for people to help her hand-sew a collection of 200 one-of-a-kind T-shirts commissioned by a major New York retailer, and the Alabama quilters were a perfect match. Mindful of the excessive waste of fabric in the fashion industry, Natalie chose to use jersey from recycled T-shirts—an environmentally conscious and readily available fabric with an inviting, well-worn feel. The demand for these garments eventually launched the company Project Alabama, which she later separated from to form Alabama Chanin.

From its 4,000-square-foot studio space in a former textile factory, Alabama Chanin continues to enlist local artisans, who are often able to do their work out of their homes in a cottage-industry fashion, to create custom garments, jewelry, and home furnishings. The use of sustainable and often quirky materials—organic cotton fabrics, natural and low-impact dyes, recycled metals, and found objects ranging from cow bones to old neckties—ensure that no two items are alike and place age-old techniques in a contemporary context. "The term sustainable design was first used to describe a way of manufacturing with materials and methods that have a low impact on the earth," explains Natalie. "It has since evolved to include the idea of sustaining traditions." She notes that people of her mother's generation tended to see less value in handmade items and considered store-bought to be better. Today, however, Natalie sees that people are beginning to understand the value, both ecologically and economically, in handmade items and the traditions behind them.

To learn more about Alabama Chanin, and to try your hand at projects designed by Natalie, pick up *Alabama Stitch Book* (Stewart, Tabori & Chang, 2008). You can also view Natalie's collection and learn about her sewing workshops on her website: www.alabamachanin.com.

Graphic Pillows

Pillows are a quick and inexpensive way to refresh your living space, especially if you repurpose fabrics and use a bold design. Choose from the three appliqué motifs given here, or come up with your own to suit your personal style.

Finished Measurements
18" square

Materials
(For one pillow)
18"-square pillow form
18" square of mid- to heavyweight fabric, such as felted wool, corduroy, or wool melton *(for front; note that for Sprout design, square pillow front is made by seaming three rectangles, 18" x 6⅜", in different colors)*
18" square of coordinating fabric, such as mid-weight print or upholstery-weight fabric *(for back)*

Coordinating pieces of wool felt for chosen appliqué that complement pillow front and back fabrics:
Sprout: Three rectangles, 7" x 11", in different colors
Leaf: Three rectangles, 5" x 17", in different colors
Flower: Rectangle, 13" x 15", in Color A; 9" square in Color B; 6" squares in Colors C and D
45"-wide double-sided fusible webbing: ¼ yard for Sprout and Leaf; ½ yard for Flower
Paper scissors
Fabric shears
Hand-sewing needle and thread coordinating with front and back fabrics
Pencil

GATHERING MATERIALS

Use repurposed materials to make the pillow cover, such as wool blankets, long skirts made of wool suiting or corduroy, and even drapery. For the appliqué accents, use fabric from felted wool sweaters (see page 138 for tips on felting wool). You can even make an eco-friendly choice when selecting your pillow form since many are now stuffed with eco-friendly fibers, such as bamboo, corn, hemp, and even fiber made from recycled water bottles (see Resources on page 141).

> **"There is no beauty in the finest cloth if it makes hunger and unhappiness."**
> MAHATMA GANDHI

❶ Prepare Pillow Front and Back

Lay out flat your fabrics for the pillow front and pillow back. With fabric shears, cut an 18" square from each fabric, which will give a snug, firm fit to the pillow cover.

Note that if you're using the Sprout appliqué design, you'll need to make the 18"-square pillow front by seaming three 18" x 6⅜" rectangles in different colors with a ¼" seam. This will produce an 18" x 18⅛" rectangle, which you can then trim by ⅛" to make an 18" square.

❷ Prepare Appliqué

Choose an appliqué design from the pullout sheet at the back of the book. Then follow the directions on page 139 for working with fusible webbing and applying the appliqué to the background fabric.

❸ Fuse Appliqué to Pillow Front

Peel away the paper backing from the back of the appliqué shapes. Place the shapes, webbing side down, onto the right side of the pillow front in your desired layout. (For the Flower appliqué, fuse one layer at a time, starting with the largest shape first.) Cover the appliqués with a press cloth, and fuse them to the pillow front with an iron, following the manufacturer's directions.

❹ Stitch Appliqués

FOR SPROUT APPLIQUÉ: Edge-stitch (see page 133) each leaf appliqué.

FOR LEAF APPLIQUÉ: Zigzag-stitch around the perimeter of the leaf shape and along the two "seams" in the leaf's center, where the appliqué edges butt together.

FOR FLOWER APPLIQUÉ: Edge-stitch each appliqué shape. Leave the small dots in the center unstitched.

❺ Assemble Pillow Cover

Lay the pillow back right side up, and lay the appliquéd pillow front right side down on the pillow back, so the fabrics' right sides face together and the edges are aligned. Pin the edges together, and straight-stitch around the perimeter with a ½" seam, leaving an opening of 10"-12" on one side and backstitching (see page 133) at both sides of the opening to reinforce it.

❻ Turn, Stuff, and Close

Clip the seam allowances (see page 140) at the pillow's corners, and turn the work right side out through the opening you left. Feed the pillow form in through the opening, starting with the corner of the form and compressing the form as much as possible. Work the corners of the form into the corners of the cover. Fold in the seam allowances at the opening, and pin them in place. With a hand-sewing needle and thread, hand-sew the opening closed with a whipstitch (see page 135).

❼ Raise Your Style Quotient

Toss your new, bold pillows onto your same-old sofa to give it a fresh, new look!

Woodland Draft Buster

With this draft buster, you can block those wintry winds that sneak through the small open spaces under doors and windows while, at the same time, adding a touch of beauty and whimsy to your home. And preventing drafts will help you refrain from cranking up the heat! Earn extra green bonus points by stuffing your draft buster with those devious plastic bags that always seem to find a way into your home, even when you're trying hard to avoid them.

Finished Measurements
4" x 36" *(width of typical exterior door)*

Materials
½ yard of 42"-wide *(or wider)* sturdy brown fabric, such as corduroy, denim, or wool suiting

Felt scraps: 8" square in green *(for leaves)*; 5" x 8" rectangle in tan *(for log ends)*; 6" x 8" rectangle in gray *(for snail body and fungi)*; and 3" x 8" rectangle in gold *(for snail shell)*

Several printed cotton scraps, at least 8" square *(for leaves; I used 4 green and brown prints)*

Double-sided fusible webbing, one 8½" x 11" sheet

All-purpose thread, in brown

Heavyweight thread, in tan or another color contrasting with brown fabric

Fabric shears

Chalk wheel or chalk pencil

Pencil

Hand-sewing needle

Fabric glue

50 to 75 plastic grocery bags, for stuffing *(thin, flimsy bags work best)*

❶ Prepare Materials
Launder the fabric, and press it if necessary. If you are repurposing a garment, cut open the seams (such as the inseam on a pair of pants), and lay the fabric flat.

❷ Cut Pattern Pieces
Photocopy the patterns on page 46, enlarging them as noted, and cut 1 Log and 1 Branch from the brown fabric. Cut 2 Log Ends, one in each size, from tan felt.

GATHERING MATERIALS

For the main fabric, try reusing an old pair of corduroy pants or wool dress pants in a dark brown stripe or plaid. For stuffing your log, try plastic shopping bags, wool felt scraps, shredded paper, recycled beanbag filler, organic wool or cotton batting, or an eco-friendly fiberfill made from corn byproducts (see Resources on page 141). I do not recommend filling the draft buster with anything that mice or bugs might enjoy, such as rice or dried beans.

❸ Stitch Wood Grain (optional)

If your brown fabric has a texture or pattern, you can skip this step and proceed to Step 4. If your fabric is plain and you want to create a tree-bark effect on it, use the chalk wheel to mark random wood grain lines and "knots" on the right side of the cut log and branch. Then thread your machine with the heavy-weight tan thread (or a contrasting color of your choice), and sew along the chalk lines to create the appearance of tree bark.

❹ Stitch Rings on Log Ends

To mimic the tree's rings on the tan-felt log ends, rethread your machine with brown all-purpose thread. Topstitch a spiral pattern on the large log end, starting at the outside edge of the circle, following the edge, and spiraling in toward the center. Repeat the process for the small log end.

❺ Assemble Log

Fold the log lengthwise with right sides together. Sew the side seam of the log (creating a tube), leaving a 6" opening in the middle of the seam. With the tube still turned wrong side out, align the large log end circle with the opening at the log's wide end. Pin the circle in place, distributing the fabric evenly around the opening. *Note: It may help to use your scissors to make ⅛" clips (see page 140) into the seam allowance of the tube's opening to help ease it around the circle. Sew the log end in place with a ¼" seam. Repeat the process with the small log end and the log's narrow end. Turn the work right side out through the center opening in the side seam.*

❻ Sew Branch

With the branch wrong side up, hem its widest end by folding it ⅛" to the wrong side and edge-stitching (see page 133) the fold. Then fold the branch lengthwise, with right sides together. Align, pin, and straight-stitch the side edges and across the narrow end with a ¼" seam. Clip the seam allowance at the corner, and turn the branch right side out.

❼ Fill 'Er Up

Starting with the log, stuff clean, dry plastic grocery bags through the opening in the side seam, stuffing both ends as firmly as possible. When the log is fully and evenly stuffed, hand-stitch the opening closed using a whipstitch (see page 135) and matching thread. Stuff the branch in a similar manner, through the wide opening.

WOODLAND DRAFT BUSTER PATTERNS

(Photocopy at 200%)

Note that, for the Log, you will cut fabric to the dimensions indicated.

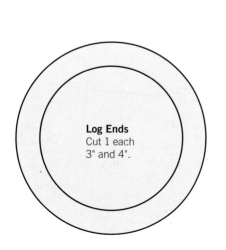

Log Ends
Cut 1 each
3" and 4".

Stitch
here.

Snail Body
Cut 1.

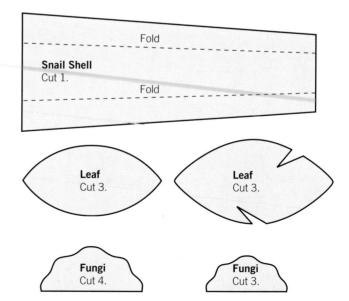

Fold

Snail Shell
Cut 1.

Fold

Leaf
Cut 3.

Leaf
Cut 3.

Fungi
Cut 4.

Fungi
Cut 3.

❽ Attach Branch

About 10" from the log's narrow end, pin the open end of the branch on the top of the log, making sure all the bag stuffing is tucked inside. Hand-stitch the branch opening to the log using a whipstitch and matching thread.

❾ Make Leaves and Fungi

Trace six leaf shapes on the paper side of a piece of fusible webbing. Following the manufacturer's directions, fuse the webbing to the wrong side of a fabric scrap with an iron. With fabric shears, cut out the shapes along the pencil lines. Peel away the paper baking; place the cut-out shapes, webbing side down, on top of a piece of green felt; and fuse the two layers together. Trim the edge of the felt, leaving a ¼" border between the felt and the printed cotton. For added detail, machine-stitch a "vein" up the center of each leaf. Repeat the cutting and fusing process for the fungi.

❿ Make Snail

Using the patterns provided, cut out the Snail Shell and Snail Body from felt scraps in your desired colors. To create the shell, fold the felt piece lengthwise (as indicated on the pattern) so that the two long sides meet. Hand-stitch the edges together with a whipstitch. Then, beginning with the widest end, fold the end in and roll it all the way to the narrow end. Hand-tack the end of the roll to secure it. To create the snail body, make a tuck in the body by pinching the sides of the felt piece together and taking a small stitch where indicated on the pattern. Next, roll the "head" (the curved end of the body) about ¾" toward the stitches you just took, and take another stitch to secure the roll in place. Attach the shell to the body and to the back of the head with fabric glue or by hand-stitching.

⓫ Attach Log Details

Decide on the placement of the decorative details and use fabric glue to attach them to the log. Apply a small bead of glue along the straight edge of the fungi, and press it into the side of the log. Make pairs of overlapping leaves, gluing the pairs together where they overlap, and then glue them to the branch and log. Apply a small amount of glue to the underside of the snail, and press it into place on top of the log. Pin each piece into place to dry.

⓬ Be Crafty, Not Drafty!

To keep warm without a fireplace, lay the finished draft buster log along the base of your drafty door or window.

36"

Log
Cut 1 with
dimensions noted.

⌊___ Place on fold ___⌋

6"

4"

Branch
Cut 1.

⌊___ Place on fold ___⌋

14¾"

Recycled Sweater Slippers

Try refashioning that worn-out wool sweater lurking in the back of your closet into a pair of warm, durable slippers. Just a quick trip through the washer and dryer will transform that well-loved woolie into a soft, dense material that can be cut up without unraveling. These slippers are a quick project that you can easily finish in a day. Reduce your CO_2 footprint by not buying factory-made, and, at the same time, make a warmer "footprint" for yourself!

Sizing

Extra Small: Kids' 1/2
Small: Kids' 3/4 or Women's 5/6
Medium: Kids' 5/6 or Women's 7/8
Large: Women's 9/10 or Men's 7/8
Extra-Large: Men's 9/10

Materials

1 or 2 large men's or women's wool sweaters with ribbing at bottom edge *(I used two sweaters in complementary colors for this project; heavy sweaters work best)*

6 to 8 yards of yarn in coordinating color *(I used fingering-weight wool, but any fiber or weight will work)*

Suede elbow patches or scraps and leather machine-needle (optional)

Fabric shears

Paper scissors

Tapestry needle

❶ Prepare Materials

Felt the sweaters following the guidelines on page 138.

❷ Cut Pieces

Photocopy the patterns on page 51, enlarging as noted, and use paper scissors to cut out the pattern in your desired size. Cut two sets of slipper uppers from the main body of the sweater, cutting two uppers with the pattern right side up and two uppers with the pattern flipped over to its reverse side (you'll make each slipper with a pair of the mirror-image uppers). Cut two soles for the slippers out of the sleeves, again flipping the pattern pieces over so that you're making a right and left sole. Finally, cut two slipper cuffs from the sweater ribbing.

❸ Grip or Slip

If the slippers will be worn on hard surfaces, such as a wood floor, I recommend adding non-slip sole grippers. I made my sole grippers from a pair of suede elbow patches from a men's jacket, but any lightweight suede or Ultrasuede scrap will do. Cut two large circles and two small circles from suede using the patterns provided on page 51. Center and pin the large suede circle on the right side of the slipper sole to the area for the ball of the foot. Pin the smaller suede circle to the heel area of the sole. Using a leather-sewing needle in your machine, carefully edge-stitch (see page 133) around each circle. Repeat the process for the other sole.

❹ Assemble Slippers

To keep the inside of these slippers as comfy as can be, construct them with the seam allowances on the outside of the slippers: With the wrong sides (what was originally the inside of the sweater) of a mirror-image pair of slipper uppers facing together, lay one upper on top of the other upper. Align and pin the slipper-upper seam and the heel seam, and machine-stitch the two seams with a ¼" seam and a long stitch length.

To attach the sole to the sewn upper, place the two pieces wrong sides together, aligning the markings on the sole, as noted on the pattern piece, to the heel and toe seams of the sewn slipper upper. Pin around the sole's edge, and machine-sew the sole in place with a ¼" seam. Repeat the process for the second slipper.

❺ Attach Cuffs

Fold the length of ribbed cuff in half, with the right sides together and the short ends aligned. Make a tube by pinning the aligned ends together and machine-sewing them with a ¼" seam. Turn the cuff right side out.

Place the cuff inside the slipper, aligning one of the cuff's edges with the slipper's top opening and the cuff's seam with the slipper's heel seam. Make sure that the right side (the outside) of the cuff faces the wrong side (the inside) of the slipper. Pin the cuff to the slipper around the edge, distributing the cuff fabric evenly; and machine-sew the cuff to the slipper with a ¼" seam. Pull the cuff to the outside of the slipper, and fold it down to create a rolled cuff that covers the seam. Repeat the process for the second slipper.

❻ Extra Sole

If you've got some extra felted wool scraps, you can boost the comfort and durability of your slippers by making an insole. Simply cut an extra set of soles to thicken the base of the slipper. Then trim ¼" off the perimeter of each insole, and slide an insole inside each slipper.

❼ Finishing Touches

At this point your slippers are ready to wear, but you may want to add some extra detail. I added decorative blanket-stitching (see page 135) around the slipper's seam allowances, using a tapestry needle and yarn in a coordinating color from my stash. You might also want to personalize your slippers by adding embroidery, needle felting, pompoms, or any other trim you might have in your bag of tricks.

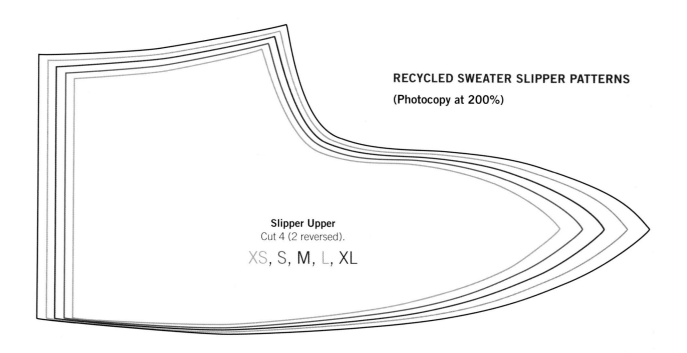

RECYCLED SWEATER SLIPPER PATTERNS

(Photocopy at 200%)

Slipper Upper
Cut 4 (2 reversed).

XS, S, M, L, XL

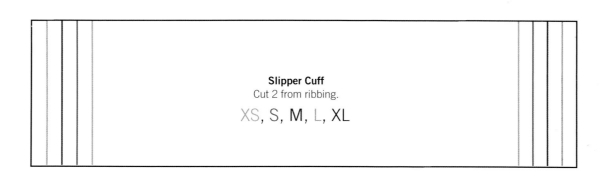

Slipper Cuff
Cut 2 from ribbing.

XS, S, M, L, XL

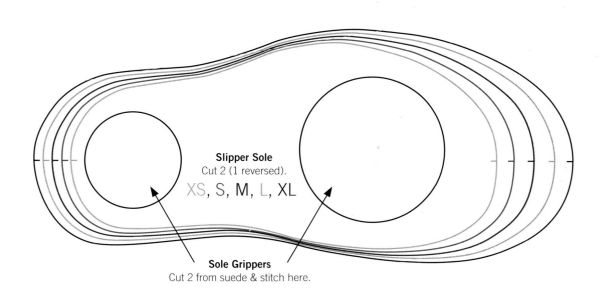

Slipper Sole
Cut 2 (1 reversed).

XS, S, M, L, XL

Sole Grippers
Cut 2 from suede & stitch here.

Felted Foliage Scarf

Sometimes common sense and fashion sense don't mix—especially in winter when you're trying to stay warm *and* be stylish. The Felted Foliage Scarf is just the answer to this conundrum. Start by felting a few wool sweaters to transform into a fresh, one-of-a-kind (re)fashion statement. The layered leaves provide texture, dimension, and warmth; and because the knitting is done for you (since you're starting with preknit sweaters) and the edges are left raw, this scarf can be whipped up quickly.

Finished Measurements
Approximately 7" x 60"

Materials
1 large wool sweater, in green
2 or 3 wool sweaters or wool felt
  scraps in brown and green shades
Several yards of thin brown yarn
Fabric shears
Chalk pencil or chalk wheel
Rotary cutter and cutting mat (optional)
18" metal-edge ruler
Tapestry needle

SOFTNESS IS KEY

When choosing sweaters to felt for this scarf, take note of their softness since you will be wearing the scarf around your neck. If the sweater is at all itchy before felting, it will still be itchy afterward.

❶ Prepare Materials
Start by deconstructing the sweater(s) for your scarf, using fabric shears and following the directions on page 8, with one exception: For this project, instead of completely separating the front from the back, cut open the shoulder seams and one side seam, leaving the body's other side seam intact. Then machine-wash and felt the sweater pieces, as explained on page 138.

Step 4
Leaf placement.

LEAF PATTERN

(Photocopy at 100%)

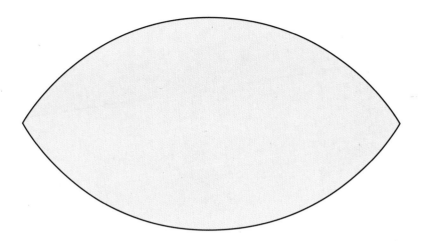

❷ Cut Scarf Strips

Lay out the body of the sweater on your work surface. To best use the fabric, cut strips across the lower body of the sweater, between the top of the waist ribbing or the hem and the underarm. With a ruler and chalk pencil, draw two parallel lines 5" apart. Cut along the lines, using fabric shears or a metal ruler, rotary cutter, and self-healing cutting mat, making the strips as long as possible. If there is enough room to cut a second 5"-wide strip from the sweater body, do so. Otherwise, lay out the sleeve fabric on your work surface, and cut a 5"-wide strip down each sleeve, from wrist to shoulder.

❸ Assemble Strips

Lay out the strips end to end to form the base of the scarf. You can join the butted ends of the strips either by machine or by hand. If you're using a sewing machine, sew the butted pieces into one long strip using a wide zigzag stitch that straddles both pieces. If hand-stitching, whipstitch (see page 135) the butted ends together using a hand-sewing needle and thread. There is no need to finish the side edges of the scarf since the felted fabric will not unravel. Repeat the process of joining the butted ends until the scarf has reached the length you want (the scarf shown is 60" long). Then press the seams flat.

❹ Foliate Your Scarf!

Using an assortment of felted sweater scraps and the Leaf Pattern above, cut out approximately 40 leaf shapes in desired colors. Don't worry if the leaves are not perfectly uniform; you're imitating nature, after all! Arrange the leaves on the scarf (see the drawing at left for the suggested placement of the leaves), and pin them in place. Thread a sharp tapestry needle with a length of yarn, and knot the end. Using a long running stitch (see page 135), hand-sew each leaf to the scarf base with a couple of stitches down the center to create the leaf's center vein. Tie off and cut the yarn under each leaf, or use a continuous strand of yarn to attach multiple leaves, as follows: After sewing the first leaf, knot the yarn under the leaf and carry it to the next leaf to be sewn. Bring the needle and yarn up to the top of the new leaf, sew a center vein, knot it under the leaf, and carry it under the leaf to the next leaf to be attached. Continue this process to sew a number of leaves with the same strand, hiding the knots and yarn carried under the leaves.

❺ Wrap and Go

Lickety-split, you've gone from cast-off sweater to cold-weather glamour! You'll feel so warm and wonderful that you'll want to make a few more scarves as gifts.

crispina
ffrench

Crispina ffrench has a knack for revealing the hidden beauty within discarded materials. As the founder and creative director of Crispina Design Workshop, her wholesale manufacturing company, Crispina turns secondhand stuff—T-shirts, wool sweaters, corduroy pants, denim jeans, men's dress shirts—into "funktional heirlooms such as pillows, rugs, and one-of-a-kind clothing. In doing so, she offers what she calls "consciousness and beauty" through the combination of recycling and art.

As a fine art major at the Massachusetts College of Art in Boston in the 1980s, Crispina funded her education by selling handmade products such as her signature Ragamuffins, whimsical creatures made from felted wool sweater scraps. "The school was not pleased with me," Crispina says. "I was frowned upon by one of my sourpuss fine-art advisors for crossing over into craft." But that attitude didn't deter her. During her senior year, when most of her classmates were learning how to make slides of their work to prepare their portfolios, Crispina continued making Ragamuffins, as well as home accessories, out of secondhand clothing and selling them to retail shops. Her favorite medium: woolen thrift-store sweaters, fulled (shrunken by washing and drying repeatedly) to achieve a feltlike consistency.

"As a developing business, it was hard to find consistent materials," she says, referring to the reclaimed wool sweaters she makes into throws, pillows, and other objects. But eventually, through a supplier, she was able to buy large quantities of used clothing from "garment graders" who sort unusable garments for rags. Crispina once ventured into using new fabrics for her designs, but though the collection was well received in the market, it was not as personally satisfying as using reclaimed materials. "It sold well, but it was not cohesive with the rest of my line," she explains. "It was for a different customer."

It is important to Crispina to keep her focus on recycling and mindful consumption, reflecting her concern for the environment. Her business began before most people even thought of reused clothing as a form of recycling—often, people even wondered if the materials were dirty because they were secondhand. But in the years since, she has noticed an attitude change. "People want a useful product that is conscientious," Crispina says.

Crispina loves making stuff, whether it's one of her sumptuous woolen throws or a colorful rug made from discarded T-shirts. She has built a business around that love and it resonates with her customers, who often find nostalgia in the recycled materials. "When someone looks at my work," she says, "a connection is made. They like the aesthetic, and they like the history. If it's a patchwork blanket with sixty-four squares, theoretically that's something that came from the lives of sixty-four people. That means something."

For more information about Crispina and her product line, visit her website at www.crispina.com.

Tyvek Tote

What can you do with those Tyvek envelopes that show up in your mailbox? Since they are made of a synthetic material, they can't be recycled with your paper products. You can always wrap them up and send them to DuPont's recycling facility (search "Tyvek recycling" on DuPont's website, www.dupont.com), but an even quicker, creative solution is to repurpose them into a lightweight and durable tote. To create this playful polka-dot design, you simply coat bubble wrap with paint and stamp it onto the mailer, effectively turning your trash into a pretty piece of printed "fabric."

Finished Measurements
Approximately 15" high x 14" wide

Materials
Four 11½" x 15", used Tyvek
   mailing envelopes
1 sheet each of large- and small-
   bubble wrap, at least 12" x 16"
Scissors
Disappearing-ink fabric marker
Paper clips
1"-wide sponge brush
Acrylic craft paint in turquoise
   and lime green
Plate or palette, for mixing paint
Newspaper

❶ Prep Envelopes

Carefully remove, if you can, any labels from the outside of the Tyvek envelopes. Crunch up the envelopes to give them an all-over crinkly texture; then smooth them flat with your hands. Turn the envelopes completely inside out, working out the corners with your fingers. Fold the flap at the opening to the inside, and press it with your hand to reseal it.

❷ Paint Dots

Spread out newspaper to protect your work surface. Lay the sheet of bubble wrap with large bubbles on the newspaper, with the bubble side facing up. On a plate or palette, mix turquoise paint with a little water to get a smooth consistency. Using the foam brush, apply paint to the bubble wrap, covering the top surface of each bubble. Lay one envelope on the painted bubble wrap, and lightly press the envelope with your hands to evenly print it, taking care not to shift the envelope as you work. Lifting the envelope up from one corner, remove it, and place it face up to dry. Repeat the process to print one side of each of the other three envelopes, and set them aside to dry. When the envelopes are fully dry, repeat this process on their opposite side using the sheet of bubble wrap with small bubbles and lime green paint. Again place the envelopes wet-paint side up, and allow them to dry.

> 66 When we try to pick out anything by itself we find that it is bound fast by a thousand invisible cords that cannot be broken, to everything else in the universe. 99
>
> **JOHN MUIR**

❸ Seam Envelopes

Lay one envelope, turquoise side up. Lay a second envelope on top of the first one, with the lime side facing down. Align and secure the two envelopes along one long side with paper clips. Then stitch the paper-clipped edges together with a ¼" seam, removing the paper clips as you sew.

Open up the work flat, with the right side facing up. Lay the third envelope with its turquoise side facing down, on top of the right side (lime) of the second envelope, aligning the long sides of these two envelopes. Secure the newly aligned long sides with paper clips, and stitch the sides together with a ¼" seam. Open up the work flat, wrong side up. Finger-press the seam allowances inward, towards the center envelope. Edge-stitch (see page 133) the seam allowances down next to original seam lines.

❹ Assemble Tote

Fold the sewn envelopes so that the right (turquoise) sides of the first and third envelopes are facing each other and the seams are aligned at the sides (the lime green-dot bag will become the bottom of the tote). Secure the long sides with paper clips, and sew the side seams of the bag with a ¼" seam.

Make a box corner by marking the bottom fold on one side of the tote with a disappearing-ink fabric marker and aligning the marked fold with one side seam to create a point at the corner (see page 138). Paper-clip the folded corner in place, and mark a line across the corner perpendicular to the marked bottom fold, 1¾" from the point. Stitch along the marked line, and repeat the process to box the other corner.

❺ Hem Top and Make Handles

With the bag still inside out, fold the edge of the top opening 1" to the wrong side, and topstitch the folded edge in place, about ⅞" from the fold.

To make handles, cut two strips from the fourth envelope, each measuring 2" x 15". With one strip laid wrong side up, fold the cut edges toward each other lengthwise, so that they meet in the center of the strip. Butt the edges together, and stitch down the center of the strip along its full length using a wide zigzag stitch to catch and secure both edges. Repeat the process for the second strip.

❻ Attach Handles

Place the ends of one handle inside the tote's top edge, about 6" apart, centering them across the width of the tote on one side and overlapping the top edge by about 1", so each end aligns with the opening's hem. Secure each end of the handle with a paper clip, making sure the strip is not twisted. Then attach each end of the handle by topstitching a square on it and stitching an X in the center of the square for reinforcement. Repeat the process to attach the second handle on the other side of the tote. Turn the tote right side out.

❼ Grab and Go

Super cute and lightweight, your trash-to-treasure tote will come in handy on many occasions. And no one will believe you when you say it came free in the mail.

Off-the-Cuff Wallet

Show your environmentalism by carrying your "green" in a wallet made out of cuffs repurposed from a man's dress shirt. Sturdy yet pliable, cuffs are easy to layer and sew together to create pockets for the multitude of cards and cash we rely on every day.

Finished Measurements
3" x 5", folded

Materials
2 men's dress shirts with following
   cuff dimensions:
Shirt A: About 3" x 10¼"
   (for outer wallet)
Shirt B: About 2½" x 10¼"
   (for inner pockets)
7" length of ⅝"-wide grosgrain
   ribbon, cut in half
2" length of ⅝"-wide Velcro
Fabric shears
Seam ripper
Disappearing ink fabric marker

tip

REPURPOSING DRESS SHIRTS

When looking in a thrift store (or in any man's closet) for shirts to repurpose, check the sleeve cuffs for excessive wear. Stay away from cuffs with frayed edges or permanent wrist grime. Sleeve cuffs vary in size, so bring along a tape measure to check dimensions. Do not use French cuffs (the kind that fold back and secure with cuff links) since they're quite large and can be very stiff.

This wallet is closed with Velcro. If you like the decorative look of the buttons that came sewn onto the shirt and want to leave them in place, beware that they may get in the way of the machine foot when sewing. Using a zipper foot attachment will help you navigate stitching close to the buttons, or, alternatively, you can remove the buttons with your seam ripper and sew them back on later.

❶ Salvage Cuffs

Using fabric shears, cut away the shirt sleeve from one cuff of Shirt A by cutting the sleeve about ½" away from the cuff edge. Using a seam ripper, gently rip open the topstitched seam across the bottom edge of the cuff, and remove the ½" strip of fabric left from cutting away the shirt sleeve. Discard the strip, and pull out any remaining loose threads. Repeat the process to remove the second cuff from Shirt A and one cuff from Shirt B.

❷ Create Inner Card Pockets

Lay one cuff from Shirt A on your work surface, with the cuff's inner side facing up. *Note: The inner side (the side originally next to the wearer's wrist) is usually soft and flexible, while the outer side is stabilized from the inside with interfacing, giving it a smooth, crisp appearance.* Lay the cuff from Shirt B on top of the Shirt A cuff, aligning the bottom edge of the two cuffs. Sew the cuffs together by topstitching across their bottom edges, ½" from the edge. Fold the stitched cuffs in half, matching the short ends, and mark the center fold with a disappearing-ink marker. Unfold the cuffs, and then topstitch along the marked center line.

Center a 3½" length of ⅝"-wide grosgrain ribbon over this row of topstitching, folding the ribbon under ¼" at each end. Pin the ribbon in place, and edge-stitch (see page 133) along each side and both ends of the ribbon through all layers.

Use the disappearing-ink marker to mark a vertical line 1" from each end of the cuffs, and topstitch along these lines.

❸ Find Closure

Separate the two sides of a 2" length of Velcro, and place one at each end of the card pockets, positioning each piece vertically between the topstitched line and the end of the cuff. Pin the Velcro pieces in place; then hand-sew or edge-stitch by machine the perimeter of the Velcro through all layers.

❹ Create Cover and Bill Pocket

Fold the second cuff from Shirt A, end to end. Find its center point, and mark the fold with a disappearing-ink fabric marker on the outside of the cuff. Center a 3½" length of ⅝"-wide grosgrain ribbon on the outside of the cuff over the marked line. Fold the ribbon under ¼" at each end. Pin the ribbon in place, and edge-stitch along each side and both ends of the ribbon through all layers.

Place the cuff, outside down, on your work surface. Lay the sewn cuffs (A and B) on top of the new cuff so that both of the Shirt A cuffs face together. Pin and stitch the cuffs together, ⅛" from the edge, along the ends and bottom edge. Leave the top edge open to create a bill pocket.

❺ Cash and Carry

Now that you're finished, fill up that wallet with all of the money you saved by making it yourself. If you're wondering what you can do with the body of the dress shirts, see the Striped Café Apron on page 14.

FUROSHIKI: AN ECO-FRIENDLY
WRAPPING TRADITION FROM JAPAN

Furoshiki is the word for the traditional wrapping cloths that the Japanese originally used to tie up and carry clothing or other goods, and their use dates back to as early as 710 AD. Today interest in furoshiki as a replacement for disposable bags and wrapping paper is growing.

Furoshiki can be made out of nearly any square piece of fabric that can be easily tied, such as cotton, silk, rayon, or nylon. You can use anything you might have around the house or pick up while thrifting, such as a scarf, napkin, or bandana, or you can simply cut cloth from your stash in the size you need. Fabric edges may be hemmed or left raw.

For best results, furoshiki cloths should be sized according to the gift you're wrapping. A good rule of thumb is to make sure that the length of the diagonal line from corner to corner of the cloth is two-thirds longer than the length of the item being wrapped. The folding technique for the basic carry wrap shown here, called Otsukai Tsutsumi, is simple.

❶ Lay out the furoshiki right-side down with the corners representing the four points of the compass.

❷ Place the gift in the center, adjusting the placement slightly toward the south according to the size of the item being wrapped (place smaller gifts farther south).

❸ Fold the south corner over the gift, tucking it in underneath if there is excess fabric.

❹ Fold over the north corner so that it hangs over the edge of the gift.

❺ Fold over the east and west corners, and tie them together in a square knot.

There are myriad folding methods to suit shapes ranging from jewelry boxes to wine bottles to watermelons. To see illustrations of different folding techniques, visit the Japanese Ministry of the Environment website (http://www.env.go.jp/en/focus/attach/060403-5.html).

When you present your gift, remind the recipient not to throw away the furoshiki, but to use it for regifting (of the very best kind!).

All-About-You Heat-Therapy Pillow

Sometimes a busy life can be a pain in the neck, which is precisely where a lot of us carry our tension. Ease your aching muscles with this soothing heat-therapy pillow. Designed with a curved shape to lie evenly across the back of the neck and shoulders, it's filled with buckwheat seeds, which are natural, hypoallergenic, and dust-free. The pillow can be heated in the microwave and also has a removable, washable cotton cover. Have fun mixing and matching fabrics—I chose a mod graphic print for one side and a snuggly organic cotton velour for the other. Now sit back and relax. You deserve it.

Materials

⅓ yard of 60"-wide organic-cotton
   muslin or sheeting
⅓ yard of 60"-wide cotton print jersey
   or broadcloth
⅓ yard of 60"-wide organic-cotton velour
Thread in a coordinating color
4" length of ½"-wide Velcro tape
1½ pounds of buckwheat groats
   or whole buckwheat seeds
   (not buckwheat hulls)
Fabric shears
Paper scissors
Paper, one 8½" x 11" sheet
   (to make funnel)
Disappearing-ink fabric marker

tip

BUCKWHEAT 101

Buckwheat groats, or seeds, are the fruit of the buckwheat plant, and they possess the special property of being able to retain heat and cold for up to 40 minutes. For a list of places where you can buy buckwheat groats, see Resources on page 141.

"That's the thing about Mother Nature, she really doesn't care what economic bracket you're in.**"**
WHOOPI GOLDBERG

HEAT-THERAPY PILLOW PATTERN

(Photocopy at 200%)

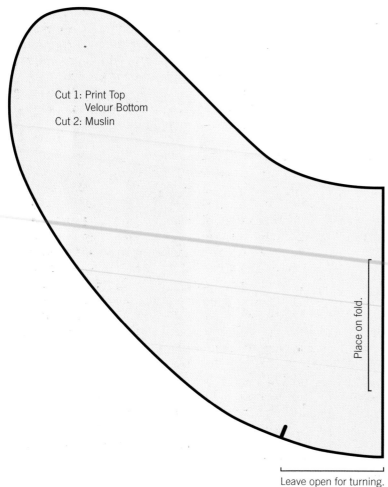

Cut 1: Print Top
      Velour Bottom
Cut 2: Muslin

Place on fold.

Leave open for turning.

❶ Prepare Materials

Prewash and -dry all the fabrics. Photocopy and enlarge the pattern provided on page 68, and cut it out with paper scissors. Using fabric shears, cut the pattern piece twice from muslin, and once each from the print fabric and the velour. With disappearing-ink fabric marker, transfer the pattern markings to the back of each cut piece.

❷ Make Inner Pillow

Place the two cut pieces of muslin together, matching and pinning their edges. Sew a ¼" seam around the muslin pillow's perimeter, leaving a 4" opening at the center back of the pillow between the pattern marks. Notch the seam allowances (see page 140) at the inner curve, and turn the pillow right side out through the opening. For reinforcement, topstitch the pillow's perimeter from the right side, excluding the center-back opening.

❸ Fill 'er Up

Make a funnel by wrapping a sheet of paper into a cone shape. Place the small end of the funnel into the pillow opening, and slowly fill the pillow with buckwheat groats, one cup at a time. Test the pillow's firmness by holding the opening closed, and laying the pillow on a flat surface. It should be about 1½" thick with the buckwheat distributed throughout

the pillow. Fold in the opening's raw edges, and topstitch (see page 133) the folded edges together to close the opening.

❹ Make Outer Pillow Cover

With the wrong side of the print pillow front facing up, fold and pin the center-back edge between the pattern marks ¼" to the wrong side. Topstitch the folded edge between the marks ³⁄₁₆" from the edge. Repeat this process for the velour pillow back.

Separate the hook and loop sides of the 4" length of Velcro tape, and sew the hook side to the hemmed area on the right side of the print pillow front, topstitching around the hook tape's four edges. Repeat this process for the velour pillow back, sewing the Velcro's loop side to the hemmed area on the wrong side.

Align the front and back pillow covers, with right sides together, and pin them in place. Starting at one end of the Velcro tape, stitch around the perimeter of the pillow with a ¼" seam. Clip the seam's allowances (see page 140) along the convex curves (the outside edge and the ends of the U-shape), and notch the seam allowances along the concave curves (inside the U-shape). Turn the pillow cover right side out, and press the seams.

❺ Assemble Inner and Outer Pillow

Hold the inner pillow by one end, allowing the seeds to empty into the opposite end of the pillow. Push the now-empty end of the inner pillow through the outer-cover's opening and down into one of its ends. With your other hand, grab the two aligned ends from the outside to hold them in place (this process is a bit like stuffing a duvet into its cover). Now lift the full end of the inner pillow, allowing about half of the seeds to shift to the empty end already inside the cover. Continue working the inner pillow into the outer cover by shifting the bulk of the seeds back and forth. After fully positioning the inner pillow in the outer cover, close the outer cover with the Velcro closure.

❻ Take the Heat

Place your heat-therapy pillow in the microwave oven, and heat it on high for no longer than two minutes. (Do a few trials to see how much time works best with your microwave.) Place the pillow on your neck and shoulders, and feel the tension melt away.

Organic Baby Quilt and Washies

Made pure and simple with organic cotton, this quilt (see right) -and-washcloth (see page 73) set is a perfect gift for new parents and their baby, and will be a cherished heirloom to pass down along with a promise for a cleaner, greener Earth. Use sweet printed fabric for both the quilt's patchwork strip and the back of the washcloths to coordinate the set.

Finished Measurements
Baby Quilt: About 29" x 34"
Washies: 8½" square

Materials

Baby Quilt
1 yard of 45"-wide organic-cotton herringbone fabric *(or other soft, woven flannel for quilt front)*
1 yard of 45"-wide organic sherpa fabric *(for quilt back; see Resources on page 141)*
1 yard of 45"-wide organic quilt batting
8 to 10 scraps of lightweight, woven-cotton prints, 5" x 3" to 5" x 6" in size, in cream, red, and tan or desired colors complementing quilt fabrics *(for patchwork detail)*
¼ yard of 30"-wide wool felt for appliqués in red or desired color
Thread in coordinating color
Cotton embroidery floss in coordinating color
Fabric shears
Rotary cutter and mat (optional)
Tapestry needle
Hand-sewing needle

Washies
(For four washies)
¼ yard of 45"-wide organic-cotton terry cloth
¼ yard of four 45"-wide lightweight woven-cotton prints (same as used for quilt's patchwork)
Felt scraps in complementary color
8" of ⅝"-wide twill tape or ribbon
Thread in coordinating
Cotton embroidery floss in coordinating color
Fabric shears
Embroidery needle
Hand-sewing needle

BABY QUILT AND WASHIE PATTERNS

(Photocopy at 100%)

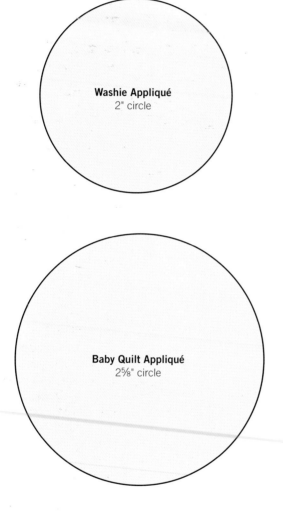

Washie Appliqué
2" circle

Baby Quilt Appliqué
2⅝" circle

BABY QUILT

❶ Prepare Materials

Machine-wash and -dry fabrics, washing like colors together and pressing the dried fabrics as needed.

❷ Make Patchwork Strip

From the fabric scraps for the patchwork, cut 8 to 10 rectangles 5" wide by 3" to 6" long, varying the lengths of the rectangles. Lay a pair of rectangles together, with right sides facing and one of their 5" edges aligned; and sew the aligned edges with a ¼" seam. Repeat the process with the rest of the rectangles to create a strip measuring 30" long. Press all the seam allowances open (see page 140).

❸ Make Quilt Front

Lay the fabric for the quilt front flat on a large work surface. Measure and cut two rectangles, one 30" x 28" and one 30" x 3". Place the patchwork strip, with right sides together, on top of the large rectangle, aligning the edge of the strip with the right edge of the rectangle. Straight-stitch the edges together with a ¼" seam, and press the seam allowances open.

Place the small rectangle on top of the patchwork strip, with right sides together, aligning the patchwork strip's raw edge and one long edge of the small rectangle. Straight-stitch the aligned edges with a ¼" seam, and press the seam allowances open. If desired, embroider a running stitch (see page 135) along the right edge of the patchwork strip, using embroidery floss and an embroidery needle.

❹ Appliqué Quilt Front

Using the larger circle pattern at left, cut out five felt circles in your desired color. Place and pin the circles in a line on the quilt front, evenly spaced and 3" from the end opposite the patchwork strip. Stitch around the circles to appliqué them either by machine (using a zigzag stitch or a decorative stitch) or by hand, using embroidery floss and a blanket stitch (see page 135). If desired, embroider a running stitch around each appliquéd circle, using embroidery floss and a tapestry needle.

❺ Cut Components

Spread out the batting and lay the quilt front, right side up, on top of the batting. Using the quilt front as a guide, cut the batting to the same dimensions. Pin and straight-stitch the batting to the wrong side of the quilt front ½" from the edges.

Spread out the sherpa fabric, right side up, on a work surface, smoothing out any wrinkles. Lay the quilt top, right side down, on top of the sherpa fabric, so the fabrics' right sides are together. Cut the sherpa fabric to the same dimensions as the quilt top, and pin around the perimeter of the two fabrics.

❻ Assemble Quilt

Stitch around the perimeter of the pinned fabrics with a ½" seam, leaving a 6" opening for turning the quilt right side out. Trim the seam allowances diagonally at the corners, and turn the work right side out through the opening. Gently push out the corners completely using the end of a chopstick. Fold in the seam allowances at the opening, and whipstitch (see page 135) them closed with a hand-sewing needle and thread. Lightly press the work if needed.

❼ Wrap it Up

After admiring your work, wrap it up as a thoughtful gift, or keep it to wrap around your own little one!

WASHIES

❶ Prepare Materials

Machine-wash and -dry the fabrics, washing like colors together and pressing any wrinkles in the dried fabrics if necessary.

❷ Cut Squares

Lay out the cotton prints on your work surface. Measure and cut four 9" squares in different prints. Then measure and cut four 9" squares in cotton terry cloth.

❸ Embellish (optional)

This washie is nice both embellished or left plain. If you want to add a circle appliqué, as in the photo at right, use the 2" circle pattern on page 72. Place the felt circle on the lower front corner of the print square, 1" above the bottom edge and 1" from the left edge. Pin the circle into place, and edge-stitch (see page 133) around it to appliqué it, either by machine (zigzag-stitching or using another decorative machine stitch), or by hand, using embroidery floss and a blanket stitch.

❹ Assemble Washie

Lay the terry-cloth square on your work surface, right side up. Cut a 2" length of twill tape for the hanger loop and fold the length in half, end to end. Align the twill tape's cut ends with the top edge of the terry square, and 1" from the left edge

of the terry square. Pin the tape's edges in place. Lay a cut woven square face down on top of the terry-cloth square (the fabrics' right sides will be together and the loop will be sandwiched between the two layers). Pin the layers together around the perimeter of the square; and straight-stitch all sides with a ¼" seam, leaving a 3" opening for turning the work right side out.

❺ Turn and Close Washie

Trim the seam allowances at the washie's corners, and turn the work right side out through the opening. Gently work out the corners with the end of a chopstick, and press the seams flat with an iron and light steam. At the opening, fold in the remaining seam allowances, and whipstitch (see page 135) the opening closed with a hand-sewing needle and thread. Machine-topstitch around the perimeter ¼" from the edges.

❻ Repeat and Rinse

Repeat steps 3 through 5 to complete all four washies. When presenting all four washies as a gift, I like to stack or roll them into a bundle, and tie the bundle with a ribbon.

Luxe Baby Hat and Toy

Secondhand never looked so sweet! Refashion a soft, buttery cashmere sweater into a unique baby gift. Both the whimsical hat and the playful pup are easily made from just one sweater. Prewashed and preshrunk, the end result is easy-care... something for moms to love, too.

Hat Sizing

Hat circumference
Newborn: 14"
6-12M: 16"
12-18M *(size shown)*: 18"
18-24M: 20"

Materials

1 women's or men's 100% cashmere sweater, preferably a L-XXL pullover
Prewashed, lightweight woven cotton, about 7" square *(for toy's ears and tail)*
Wool-felt scraps: about 3½" x 8" red rectangle *(for spot, nose, and tufts)*; about 2" brown square *(for eyes)*
2 to 4 ounces fiberfill
18" of ⅝"-wide grosgrain ribbon
Embroidery floss
Embroidery needle
Fabric shears
Disappearing-ink fabric marker or chalk wheel
Sewing needle and thread in coordinating color

tip

CHOOSING A SWEATER

You can use either a textured or smooth cashmere sweater for this project. The hat and toy shown here were sewn from a ribbed sweater, but a small cabled knit or a flat knit would work well, too.

Also be sure to save your seams! When deconstructing a cashmere sweater for fabric, trim away any seam allowance "ridges" (seen from the inside of the sweater) and set them aside. These come in handy later for creating decorative details, such as the fringe on the baby hat.

BABY HAT

❶ Prepare Materials

Using fabric shears, remove the sleeves from the sweater by cutting around the armhole. Cut the sleeve open by cutting down the underarm seam to the cuff. Machine-wash the sweater body and sleeves with detergent in hot water, and machine-dry them on a low setting. This will shrink the sweater slightly and make it softer and fluffier. If the pieces are wrinkled, lightly press them with a steam iron set on the wool setting.

❷ Cut Out Hat

Open up the body of the sweater by cutting along one of the side seams. Lay the sweater flat on your work surface. With a disappearing-ink marker or chalk wheel, measure and mark a rectangle 18" wide x 9" high (or, for a different size, refer to the sizing information on page 74, and use the circumference measurement for the rectangle's width; the rectangle's height will be 9" for all sizes), placing the rectangle's widest measurement along a finished edge of the sweater fabric, such as a waistband. If the front or back of the sweater is not wide enough to accommodate this measurement, center the rectangle on one of the sweater's side seams. Using fabric shears, cut out the rectangle.

❸ Appliqué Hat Front

Cut a circle out of red felt for the appliqué, using the pattern on page 79. To find the placement for the appliqué, fold the hat rectangle in half, matching up the short sides. With the short sides positioned on the right, measure down 1" from the center of the top edge, and align the top of the circle appliqué with this mark. Pin the circle into place, open out the rectangle flat, and stitch around the circle either by machine (using a zigzag stitch or a decorative stitch), or by hand using a blanket stitch (see page 135) and embroidery floss. If you want, embroider a running stitch (see page 135) around the circle, using embroidery floss and an embroidery needle.

❹ Make Fringe Tufts

Using fabric scraps, felt, or "sweater seams," cut 12 to 20 strips ¼" wide x 2" long. Gather 6 to 10 strips together, and secure the ends by hand-stitching them together with needle and thread to form a fringed tuft. Repeat the process to make a second tuft.

❺ Assemble Hat

Fold the hat rectangle in half, with right sides together, matching its short sides again. Place a tuft at each top corner of the square, sandwiching the tufts between the layers. Pin the sewn ends of the tufts in place, allowing the fringed ends of the tufts to hang freely *inside* the hat. Pin across the top edge of the square and down the side, stopping 2½" from the bottom edge for the cuff. *Note: If the sweater piece you're using has a ribbed band, use this as your cuff and stitch down to the ribbed area, stopping when you come to it.* Stitch across the top and side of the hat with a ¼" seam, stopping at the 2½" mark; and turn the work right side out. Pin the remaining 2½" of the side together, and stitch the pinned length with a ¼" seam from the right side. Fold back the cuff to hide the seam allowances of the last 2½".

❻ Warm Noggin

Find a sweet little baby bean to warm and snuggle with the softest hat ever!

TOY

❶ Prepare Materials

Follow Step 1 of the directions for the Baby Hat on page 77. If you're using the same sweater to make the puppy toy, often the sleeves will be large enough to use for it.

❷ Cut Out Parts

Enlarge the pattern on the facing page, as indicated, and cut 2 body pieces from the sweater sleeves, reversing the pattern to cut the second piece, so you have two mirror-image bodies. Also cut 2 ears from the sweater, without reversing the pattern. Using a coordinating lightweight woven fabric, cut 2 ears and 2 tails, reversing the pattern for each to make the second cut a mirror image of the first. Cut 2 eyes from the brown felt scrap and 1 nose and 1 spot from the red felt scrap.

❸ Sew Ears and Tail

With right sides together, align and pin the two fabric tails together. Sew the tail's curved sides with a ¼" seam, leaving the short end open. Clip the seam allowances (see page 140) on the tail's curves, and turn the tail right side out. Stuff the tail with fiberfill, using a chopstick to push fiberfill into its tip.

With right sides together, align and pin together a sweater ear and a woven fabric ear. Then sew around the pair with a ¼" seam, leaving the ear's short end open. Clip the seam allowances on the ear's curves, and turn the ear right side out. Finger-press the ear flat. Repeat the process for the second ear.

❹ Sew Puppy

Lay one body piece right side up. Place and pin the tail at the marked position on the body pattern, with the tail's open side at the seam line. Place and pin the ears side by side at the marked positions on the head, with the ears' open edges positioned at the seam line. The woven-fabric side of one ear (it doesn't matter which one) should face up, while the sweater side of the other ear should face down.

Align the second body piece, right side down, on top of the first one, sandwiching the tail and the ears inside the pieces (nothing should stick out beyond the edges of the puppy's body). Pin around the perimeter of the body, through all layers. Sew around the body with a ¼" seam, leaving a 3" opening for turning the work along the bottom of the dog behind the back foot. Clip the seam allowances along the curves, and turn the work right side out.

❺ Stuff with Fluff

Stuff the toy with fiberfill, using small pieces of stuffing one at a time and working them into the head, feet, and other tight corners in the dog's body (use a chopstick or another long tool to push the fiberfill into the corners, if needed). When you've finished stuffing, close the 3" opening by hand, using a needle, coordinating thread, and a whipstitch (see page 135). Fold one ear to each side and hand-tack the base of each ear to the head.

❻ Add Detail

Pin the eyes, nose, and spot in place as desired or following the placement marks shown on the pattern. Whipstitch or blanket-stitch these details in place using a needle and coordinating embroidery floss. Add a French knot (see page 135) highlight in the center of the eye. Add a running stitch around the spot and the eye to coordinate with the appliqué on the Baby Hat. As an optional detail, add a bow at the neck by first securely tacking the ribbon to the neck before tying it in a bow. *(Please note: For safety purposes, be sure to securely sew the ribbon to the toy, and do not use buttons for eyes since they're not safe for children's toys.)*

❼ Snuggle Up

Combine this luxe pup with the luxe baby hat for a sweet and soft baby gift that's thoughtful and conscientious.

BABY HAT AND TOY PATTERNS

(Photocopy at 133%)

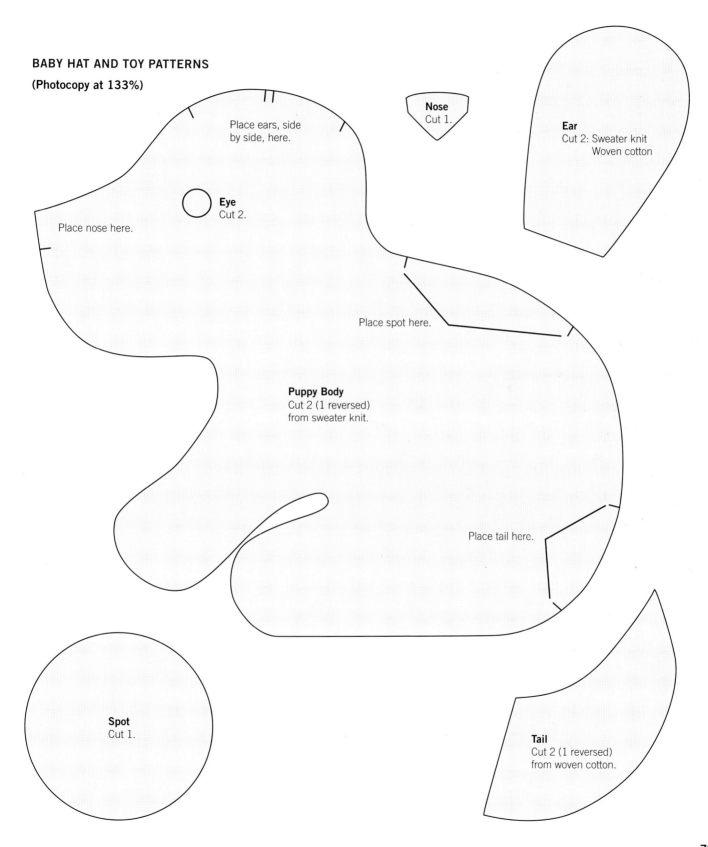

Place ears, side by side, here.

Nose
Cut 1.

Ear
Cut 2: Sweater knit
Woven cotton

Place nose here.

Eye
Cut 2.

Place spot here.

Puppy Body
Cut 2 (1 reversed)
from sweater knit.

Place tail here.

Spot
Cut 1.

Tail
Cut 2 (1 reversed)
from woven cotton.

Reversible Wrap Skirt

Some table linens are just too cute to be worn by the furniture. Take this yellow floral tablecloth I found at my LTS (local thrift shop). It just had summer skirt written all over it. That and a few stains. But not to worry! This multiseamed pattern is just right for negotiating around fabric flaws—plus it's quick to sew and easy to custom-fit. It can be made from tablecloths, tea towels, sheets, or a combination of favorite fabrics from your stash. The waistband is a simple construction of grosgrain ribbon with a D-ring closure. Best of all, it's two skirts in one. You can reverse it to another print on the flip-side!

Sizing
Small: 6/8
Medium: 10/12
Large: 14/16
Length, waist to hem, for all sizes: 22"

Materials
1 lightweight tablecloth, at least 48" square
    (for outer skirt)
1½ yards of plain-weave printed cotton fabric,
    like cotton calico or broadcloth (for lining)
4 yards of ⅞"-wide grosgrain ribbon
1 pair of 1" D-rings
Fabric shears

TABLECLOTH COUTURE

When refashioning a vintage tablecloth, look for a "cutter" (a vintage fabric not in mint condition but perfect for repurposing). Tablecloths with no flaws tend to be more expensive, so cutters offer an affordable alternative. Inspect the fabric carefully to be sure that most of it is not overly worn, faded, or stained, and eyeball whether or not you can work around the trouble spots and yield enough usable fabric for your pattern. If you select an item with a few small stains, don't assume they will wash out. The best prints for this skirt project are those with a repeating pattern or scattered motifs. Avoid patterns with heavy borders and straight lines since they won't be compatible with the curved shape of the skirt's gores.

You can also easily make this skirt from regular yardage: Simply cut seven gores (using the pie-shaped pattern on the pullout sheet at the back of the book) from one or a combination of several fabrics. To use tea towels (measuring at least 22" long), place the pattern piece vertically along the towel's center. Match the grain line marked on the pattern piece with the fabric's grain line.

❶ Prepare Fabrics

Prewash and -dry all fabrics before starting. To prevent accidentally using a damaged part of the fabric, mark any holes or permanent stains with masking tape before cutting.

❷ Cut Out Pattern

Using the gore pattern provided on the pullout sheet at the back of the book, cut seven gores from the outer skirt fabric and seven gores from the lining fabric. It is important to plan out the placement of each piece before cutting. Keep the grain line (see page 139), marked on the pattern piece, aligned with either the fabric's straight grain or its cross grain. Pay special attention to the location of flaws when placing the pattern pieces, either cutting around flaws or placing them in inconspicuous areas. It's a good idea to trace all the pieces on your fabric with a disappearing-ink marker before cutting to be sure of your placement. Because a particular vintage tablecloth is not easily replaced, you only get one chance to cut.

❸ Assemble Skirt

With right sides together, machine-stitch the long edges of the seven outer-fabric gores together with a ½" seam (but be sure to leave the edges of the two outermost gores un-sewn so that the skirt can wrap around the body). Repeat the process for the lining. Press open all seam allowances (see page 140) on both the outer skirt and the lining.

With the fabrics' right sides together, pin the outer skirt and lining together, matching the edges. Machine-stitch around the skirt's entire perimeter, using a ¼" seam and leaving an 8" opening for turning the work right side out. Notch the seam allowances (see page 140) along the waistline and hem the curves. Then turn the skirt right side out, working out the corners with your fingers. Press the edges, and edge-stitch (see page 133) the entire perimeter, closing as you sew the 8" opening you left for turning.

❹ Create Waistband

Layer two 2-yard lengths of grosgrain ribbon, one on top of the other. Edge-stitch the ribbons together down the length of one side. With the layered ribbon's front facing you and the stitched edge at the top, fold under the ribbon's right end ¼" to the wrong side, and topstitch across the folded edge. Thread both D-rings together onto the right end of the ribbon; and fold back and pin the ribbon's stitched end in place, creating a small loop around the rings. Topstitch the ribbon's end in place using a zipper foot to get as close to the flat part of the rings as possible.

❺ Attach Waistband

With the skirt right side up, insert the top right corner of the skirt between the layers of the ribbon waistband as close as possible to the D-rings. Pin the edge at the corner to secure it, and continue sandwiching the skirt into the waistband and pinning the ribbon in place until the entire top edge of the skirt is enclosed. (A length of ribbon will extend beyond the skirt's top corner at the left.) Stitch across the ribbon's short end, near the D-rings; and edge-stitch along the ribbon's lower edge, sewing through both layers of the ribbon and the skirt in-between. Stitch up across the short width of the ribbon at the top left corner of the skirt.

❻ Finish Waistband

Edge-stitch closed the ribbon-tie's remaining length. Trim the ribbon's free end at a 45-degree angle, and stitch across the angled cut to reinforce it. Measure and mark the waistband 10" in from the skirt's top left corner. At that marked position, make a 1" vertical buttonhole for the ribbon tie to pass through.

❼ Wear It Well

Wrap the skirt around your waist, overlapping the right front over the left front. Wrap the tie from the left front behind your back inside the skirt. Pass the tie's free end out through the buttonhole from the inside. Bring the tie around to the D-rings, and pull it through to secure it.

REPURPOSING ON THE BIG SCREEN

From the hip crafting crowd that restyles used clothing to the tech-geeks that hack electronics to make into homemade gadgets, the word "repurpose" is key to the DIY movement. While repurposing has deep roots in our early American history, from using feedsacks for fabric (see page 127) and scraps of wool for penny rugs (see page 22), many of us modern-day sewers can thank a few classic movies for our first exposure to the brilliance of repurposing.

It's entirely possible that the *Gone with the Wind* American icon, Scarlett O'Hara, was the first to set the trend when she looked to her own green velvet drapes for inspiration and had Mammy create a fashionable frock suitable for a Southern belle. I loved her resourcefulness and eye for style! (And, depending on your age, you may also remember Carol Burnett's hilarious parody of that scene, in which she wears not only the drapes but the curtain rod and rings, too.)

In the 1960s, *The Sound of Music* brought us the endearing governess Maria, who was inspired to refashion curtains into play clothes for the Von Trapp children. Ingenious! Although I consider myself able to use materials on hand creatively, my windows are currently covered with mini-blinds —not exactly ideal for children's clothing (although they might come in handy for a Halloween costume down the road).

Fast-forward to the 1980s classic, *Pretty in Pink*, starring Molly Ringwald as the new-wave misfit, Andie Walsh. Poor but fashion-conscious, she is inspired to refashion two secondhand dresses into a "new" pink prom dress. While not entirely a case of "art imitating life," the prom dress remake totally resonated with creative teenagers across the country.

harmony art
organic
design

When Harmony Susalla was a child, she designed her own greeting cards, complete with a "Harmony Art" label and a hand-drawn copyright symbol on the back. "That may have been an odd thing to do as a kid," she laughs. But it's not so odd when you consider that it eventually became the name of her own textile design company, Harmony Art Organic Design, where she combines her love of art with her concern for the environment through her line of printed organic cotton fabric.

Harmony studied human services in college and began a career in financial planning, eventually becoming a vice president at a large investment company. Although the position was lucrative, she was she knew it was not her calling. A chance conversation with her cousin about the California School of Professional Fabric Design in Berkeley, gave her the "aha" moment she needed to change her course, and she began to study textile design. Working full-time while attending design school nights and weekends, she earned her degree, then abandoned her VP position and began designing pajama prints for a lifestyle and sleepwear company. Before long, she was seeing her work in large department stores like Macy's and Nordstrom. Later, when she was working for a small start-up textile design company, her designs landed a major account with a big-box retailer.

Harmony's next few years were an exciting ride of design success. She loved creating patterns and designs and seeing them develop from idea to finished product. But a job offer from a competitor got her thinking: What's the next step of my career? "It was really a wake-up call," she says. "I asked myself, 'What will be my life's work?' I knew I was supposed to be doing something more meaningful."

Harmony had always been concerned about the environment. She had asked her employer about the environmental and social practices of the manufacturers that made their products. "I never really felt settled with their answers," she says. "Then one day I went into one of the stores that carried my designs to research what kinds of things they were selling. When I looked at the mass quantities of poorly made items, made by who knows who—I only saw landfill." She realized that she was indirectly contributing to the world's environmental problems. "I wanted to feel good about what I was doing," Harmony says. "I wanted to create things to be cherished rather than simply create more landfill."

Her concerns led her to research sustainable, environmentally friendly textiles. At a conference held by the Organic Trade Association, for example, Harmony learned that conventionally grown cotton uses approximately 25 percent of the world's insecticides and more than 10 percent of the pesticides. Organic cotton, on the other hand, is grown without such chemicals, using methods that have a low impact on the environment. This reality drove Harmony to seek out eco-friendly companies that she could feel good about working for. After meeting with several people in the organic fabric business, Harmony discovered that there was a shortage of printed organic fabrics in the market—which she describes as dominated by shades of oatmeal. With this realization, she figured out her next step and discovered her life's work. "I had come to a point in my career where I was ready to create the change I needed to see in our industry," Harmony says. "The job of organic textile designer didn't exist, so I had to create it."

In 2005, Harmony began her own line of organic printed cotton fabric, Harmony Art Organic Design, bringing color and style to the organic fabric market. Her work has won praise from eco-conscious interior designers looking for stylish and sustainable textile solutions as well as from manufacturers of organic baby apparel and bedding.

Living in northern California, Harmony finds inspiration in the natural beauty of her surroundings. She conveys her love of the environment through a line characterized by florals, graphic shapes, and beautiful color combinations. Harmony also raises environmental awareness about textiles by lecturing around the country and through her informative website. She points out that the Industrial Revolution was essentially launched by the textile industry. "If fabrics can launch one revolution, why not another?" she says. "We are capable of a Green Revolution."

To learn more about Harmony and where to buy her fabrics, visit her website at www.harmonyart.com.

Lunch Tote

Have you ever noticed how much trash you can generate when you get food to go? When you bring your own lunch, you make the packaging choices and can, in the process, create less waste. Make your "brown bag" green with this lunch tote in beautifully printed organic fabric. And don't forget the sandwich wraps on page 90, and even the cloth napkins on page 24.

Finished Measurements
Approximately 10" square

Materials
⅓ yard of 45"-60"-wide printed organic-cotton sateen (for outer bag)

⅓ yard of 42"-wide woven PUL (for lining; fabric laminated with polyurethane on one side to waterproof it)

⅓ yard of 45"-wide Pellon fusible fleece

24" of double-folded, extra-wide bias tape

44" of 1"-wide grosgrain ribbon

44" of ⅝"-wide striped ribbon (optional)

9" length of ¾"-wide Velcro tape

Thread in coordinating color

Fabric shears

Disappearing-ink fabric marker

tip

LINING FABRIC

Using a waterproof fabric to line this tote makes it easy to clean with a damp cloth. However, the tote is not really waterproof because of the stitched seams (through which liquids can seep). I recommend that you line your tote with PUL, or polyurethane-coated fabric. Alternatively, you can use a fabric with an acrylic coating. See Resources on page 141 for suppliers.

❶ Cut and Fuse Fabrics

Cut two panels 11" wide x 12" long, from the cotton, lining, and fusible fleece. To provide stability and insulation for the bag, fuse the fleece to the wrong side of the cotton outer-bag fabric with an iron, following the manufacturer's instructions.

❷ Sew Outer Bag and Lining

Place the two outer bag panels right sides together. Pin the 12"-long sides and 11"-wide bottom, and sew the three edges together using a ¼" seam. With the bag still wrong side out, fold the bag so that the bottom seam aligns with one of the side seams, creating a point at the corner (see Boxing a Corner on page 138). Pin the bottom and side seam together at the corner; and, using a disappearing-ink marker, mark a line perpendicular to the bottom seam, 2½" from the point. Stitch along the marked line, and repeat for the other corner. To reduce bulk, trim off the corners ¼" away from your stitching line. Repeat this process for the lining (Note: The coated side of the lining fabric is the right side).

❸ Assemble Bag

Turn the outer bag right side out. Leave the lining wrong side out. Slide the lining down inside the outer bag, aligning the side seams and bottom corners. Pin the outer bag and lining along the top edge, distributing the lining evenly around the top of the bag. Trim any excess lining, if necessary, to make the top edge even.

❹ Bind Bag's Top Edge

Unfold the 24"-long, double-fold bias tape, and follow the directions on page 137 to bind the top edge of the tote.

❺ Create Ribbon Tabs

To create ribbon tabs, cut two 4" lengths of 1"-wide grosgrain ribbon. (I layered and topstitched an additional ⅝"-wide striped ribbon on top of the grosgrain ribbon for extra detail. You can make yours simple or fancy.) Fold one length of ribbon in half, end to end, and zigzag-stitch across the raw edges to secure them. Repeat for the second tab.

Find the bag's center front and center back, halfway between the side seams, and mark these points with a pin. Position the tabs inside the top edge of the bag centered over these marks with ¾" of the tabs extending above the binding. Pin the tabs in place.

❻ Add Velcro Tape

Separate the hook and the loop sides of the 9" length of Velcro tape. Pin one side on the lining, ⅛" below the binding with the ends ½" from each of the bag's side seams (sandwich the ribbon-tab ends between the Velcro tape and the lining). Before stitching, be sure your bobbin thread matches the bag's outer fabric, since you will be stitching from the inside of the bag, which means that the bobbin thread will show on the bag's right side.

This is one of those slow, bulky steps, so take your time! Working on the inside of the bag, stitch one side of the tape, about ⅛" from its edge, removing the pins as you go. Then stitch the other edge and the ends of the Velcro. Repeat this process for the other side of the bag with the remaining Velcro tape.

❼ Make Handle

Note: The following measurements will make a short handle for your lunch tote, as shown in the photo at left. A short handle is easy to hold on to and doesn't get in your way, but if you'd prefer a longer strap that fits over your shoulder, you can easily customize the handle.

Cut two 20" lengths of grosgrain ribbon. Layer one length on top of the other, and edge-stitch (see page 133) each edge, from one end to the other, to create a double-layer ribbon. (I also layered and edge-stitched an extra ⅝"-wide striped ribbon on top of the double-layer grosgrain ribbon for extra detail.) Fold under one end of the layered ribbon ⅝", and edge-stitch the edge in place. Then fold this edge again ⅝" to the wrong side, and edge-stitch it. Repeat the process to finish the ribbon's other end.

Pin one end of the ribbon to the outside of the bag at the side seam, just below the binding. Topstitch a 1"-wide square at the end of the ribbon handle, sewing through all layers. Attach the other end of the handle in the same manner.

❽ Do Lunch

Now pack a lunch that is not only healthy for you but also healthy for the environment!

Reusable Sandwich Wraps

Make lunch, not trash! These fun, functional sandwich wraps give you a reusable alternative to plastic baggies, plus they are a snap to make. After each use, they can be wiped clean with a damp cloth or tossed in with the rest of the laundry.

Finished Measurements
7" x 14½"

Materials
⅓ yard of 45"-wide woven PUL
   (polyurethane laminated fabric; see Resources on page 141)
1" length of ¾"-wide Velcro tape
Thread in coordinating color
Fabric shears
Ruler

❶ Cut Pieces
Using the patterns provided on page 92, cut 1 Main Wrap and 2 Flaps from PUL.

❷ Hem Edges
Beginning with the main wrap, with the wrong (coated) side facing up, fold ¼" on one of the short, angled edges to the wrong side, and topstitch the fold ³⁄₁₆" from the edge. Then fold the five other short edges ¼" to the wrong side, and topstitch the fold ³⁄₁₆" from the edge, leaving the two remaining long sides unhemmed. For each rectangular flap piece, hem two short sides and one long side in the same way.

❸ Attach Flaps
With right sides together, align and pin the unhemmed edge of one flap with one of the main wrap's two unhemmed edges, centering the flap on the edge; then join the two with a ¼" seam. Fold the flap to the wrong side of the main wrap, so the wrong sides of the two pieces face together. Finger-press the fold, and topstitch the folded flap ³⁄₁₆" from the edge of the fold, encasing the seam allowances inside the fold, and backstitching (see page 133) to secure the beginning and end of your stitching. *Note: Since the side of the main wrap is a little longer than the flap's side, you will be hemming the last ½" of the main wrap's unhemmed edge as you topstitch the flap ³⁄₁₆" from the edge.* Repeat the process for the second flap and the main wrap's other unhemmed edge.

❹ Attach Velcro Tape
Separate the hook side from the loop side of the 1" piece of Velcro tape, and pin one piece to the wrong side at one end of the main wrap, following the placement noted on the pattern. Topstitch around the perimeter of the tape, and then stitch diagonally across the tape in both directions to create an X in the center. Place the remaining tape half on the other end of the main wrap on the right side, topstitch around the perimeter of the tape, and then stitch diagonally across the tape to create an X in the center.

❺ Flap, Wrap, and Go!
Lift the flaps. Place your sandwich in the center of the main wrap, and allow the flaps to overlap on top. Fold in the sides, and secure with the Velcro closure. Done!

REUSABLE SANDWICH WRAP PATTERNS

(Photocopy at 200%)

9½"

4¾"

Flap
Cut 2.

14¾"

7"

Main Wrap
Cut 1.

Velcro

Velcro

10½"

GREEN SEWING SPACES

Here are a few ways to make your sewing space environmentally friendly.

SEWING MACHINE

Using a quality sewing machine can make all of the difference when it comes to successful sewing. However, "quality" doesn't have to mean new. Consider buying a used or reconditioned sewing machine, which can often be found locally through Craigslist.com, or at your local sewing machine repair shop.

LIGHTING

Make use of natural light by putting your sewing table near a window and painting your walls a light color, so they will reflect sunlight during the day and you'll need less wattage to light the room in the evening. When possible, use task lighting that concentrates light where you want it instead of overhead or background lighting, and use compact fluorescent lightbulbs that replicate daylight (which is important for seeing colors accurately). This type of eco-friendly bulb uses 75 percent less energy and lasts ten times longer than a standard incandescent bulb.

WALLS

If you're spiffing up your space with a coat of paint, choose a low-VOC paint (VOCs are volatile organic compounds that are released into the environment every day and contribute significantly to poor indoor air quality). Most paint manufacturers now produce low-VOC or non-VOC varieties of paint, which are durable, cost-effective, and less harmful to human and environmental health than traditional wall paints.

STORAGE

Organizing your fabric stash can be tricky, and is made even more challenging if you're trying to avoid what I call plastic-bin syndrome. Use your imagination to come up with eco-smart storage solutions. Here are a few of mine to get you started: Add shelves inside an armoire for stashing fabrics and supplies. Make your own bins by covering cardboard boxes with decorative paper or fabric. Attach casters to old drawers, and roll them under your cutting table for easy access.

Denim Shopper

Carrying your own bags to the store is one of the easiest ways to be green. Refashioned from a sturdy denim skirt, this bag is easy to construct since much of the work is already done for you. Start with a long skirt in any size—the extra length is used to create the outside pockets, which are handy for stashing more reusable bags, such as the Natural Produce Bags on page 100. The original skirt pockets are great for holding onto your cell phone, keys, or shopping list. Add some comfy straps and a few appliqués for color and whimsy, and you're ready to answer "neither" to the question, "Paper or plastic?"

Finished Measurements
Approximately 15" high x 17" wide

Materials
Denim skirt, at least 26" long
   (I prefer 5-pocket jeans to maximize
   on ready-made pockets)
Fabric scraps for appliqué, preferably with
   large floral motif (those shown are
   4"–6" in diameter)
2 belts made of nylon webbing or canvas
   (mine were 2" wide x 34" long)
Heavy cotton thread matching skirt's topstitching
Double-sided fusible webbing,
   two 8½" x 11" sheets
Paper scissors
Fabric shears
Disappearing-ink fabric marker
Pencil
Heavy-duty jeans machine-needle
Old toothbrush (for fraying appliqué's edges)

tip

SEWING DENIM

Machine-sewing denim can be a challenge due to the fabric's weight. Be sure to use a new, sharp, heavy-duty jeans needle in your sewing machine, and replace the needle if it becomes damaged. Use a long stitch length and heavy cotton thread. Sew slowly, and manually turn the sewing machine's fly wheel, if necessary, when stitching over heavy seams.

❶ Prepare Main Compartment

If your skirt has a slit up the front or back, pin and topstitch the slit closed, using a long straight stitch and heavy cotton thread matching the skirt's existing topstitching. If your skirt is a lot longer than 26", cut off the excess length and re-hem it by turning its bottom raw edge ½" to the wrong side and topstitching the folded edge.

❷ Plan Pockets and Frayed-Edge Appliqués

Use a pencil to trace two or more of the appliqué fabric scrap's large flower motifs on the fusible webbing, reversing the images if they're asymmetrical. Here's how: Cover the motifs with the fusible webbing, and trace them onto one side of the webbing's translucent paper backing. Flip the traced webbing over to the other side, place it on a light box or tape it to a window, and trace the reversed images on the second side of the translucent paper backing. Cut out the webbing shapes on the traced lines on the second (reversed) side; peel away the paper backing on the first side; and position these shapes, paperless webbing side down, on the wrong side of the fabric scrap flowers. Fuse the webbing to the flowers following the webbing manufacturer's instructions. Cut out the fused fabric flowers, leaving ¼" of extra unfused fabric around each motif, so you can fray this edge.

Fold up the bottom of the skirt about 9"-10" to the right side (but don't position the hem past the bottom of the fly). Lay out your flowers on the skirt's overlap (which will become two pockets) to decide on their placement. Then peel away the remaining paper backing on the webbing; place each motif, paperless webbing side down, on the skirt's overlap. Fuse each flower to the overlap following manufacturer's instructions. Unfold the overlap, and turn the whole skirt wrong side out. Topstitch around each flower, ¼" from the edge. To fray the appliqués' raw edges, spritz them with water and brush them gently with a stiff-bristled brush, such as an old toothbrush.

❸ Make Outer Pockets

Turn the skirt right side out, and refold the bottom of the skirt about 9"-10" to the right side again. Pin the overlap evenly around the skirt, aligning each skirt seam with itself. With the skirt positioned over the arm of the sewing machine (so you're just stitching through one layer of the skirt and the overlap), start at the bottom fold and straight-stitch perpendicular to this fold along each of the skirt's original seams at the center front, center back, and both side seams. When stitching together any flat-felled seams (for example, along

> **"You must be the change you wish to see in the world."**
> MAHATMA GANDHI

the skirt's back slit), stitch along each side of the seam rather than on top of the thick seam itself. For extra durability, backstitch (see page 133) at the top of each pocket. *Note: Don't worry if your skirt has a bit of a flared hem. This will add a little fullness to your outside pockets, making them roomier.*

❹ Construct Bottom

Turn the skirt wrong side out, and pin the front and back together along the folded bottom edges. For ease of sewing, offset the center-front and -back seams slightly from each other so that they're side by side rather than stacked one on top of the other.

At this point, you'll notice that the side seams of the original skirt are not exactly at the sides of the bag. This is because the back of the skirt was made wider than the front. Ignore this difference, and mark a line with a disappearing-ink fabric marker to designate the new "side seams." Straight-stitch the pinned bottom folds together, sewing from new "side seam" to "side seam." Reinforce this seam by stitching it a second time.

❺ "Box" Corners

With the bag still wrong side out, fold it so that the bottom seam aligns with the marked "side seam," creating a point at the corner. Pin the aligned seams together, and mark a line perpendicular to the bottom seam, 1½" from the point. Stitch along the marked line, and repeat for the other corner. (For more information on boxing a corner, see page 138.) Turn the bag right side out.

❻ Measure Straps

Decide how long you want your straps to be (my finished straps are each 32"). Using fabric shears, cut the buckle off each of your belts. Measure your desired strap length, and cut each belt to this measurement, steering clear of any remaining hardware, such as grommets. If your belts are made of a synthetic fabric, like nylon webbing, you may want to "finish" the cut ends by lighting a match and carefully singeing them to prevent fraying. Otherwise, you could simply edge-stitch (see page 133) the ends to prevent unraveling.

❼ Attach Straps

Pin the ends of each strap to the outside of the skirt waistband on either side of the belt loops, at least 6" apart. Be sure the straps are not twisted. Topstitch the strap ends to the waistband by stitching a square the width of the belt over each end, then stitching an X inside the square. Repeat the process to attach all four strap ends to the waistband.

❽ BYOB

Now you're all set to BYOB (Bring your Own Bag), and kick the plastic-bag habit.

mors bags

Claire Morsman, founder
of Morsbags.com, has
always hated what humans
can unthinkingly do to
animals and the environ-
ment. Morsbags.com,
a nonprofit project aimed
at eliminating the use
of plastic bags by making
and distributing reusable
cloth ones, is a natural
development of Claire's
concern for animals and
her love of nature.

A teacher of English as a foreign language by trade, Claire lives on a houseboat in London. "I see endless plastic bags float by, and I realize that people throw them in, completely unaware of where their rubbish could end up," she explains as she begins to tell the story of how Morsbags.com came to be. It was back in 2007. She was compelled to research how marine wildlife might be affected by the bags and discovered a story about a dead Minke whale that had washed up in Normandy, France, with its stomach full of them. "That was it," says Claire. "I knew I had to do something immediate and on a personal level." When inspiration for Morsbags struck, she quickly phoned her mother to ask her to design a simple bag right away. She then asked her fiancé to create a website to spread news of her plan.

The mission of Morsbags.com is to get people together in sociable sewing groups, or "pods," to make reusable cloth bags out of cast-off fabric, such as old duvet covers, curtains, and other remnants, and then distribute them free to the unsuspecting public in line at grocery stores and through mailboxes, as well as to friends and relatives. Claire calls this approach "social guerrilla bagging," and so far, it's making an impact. To date, Morsbaggers in more than 400 pods worldwide have stitched and distributed more than 17,000 cloth bags, potentially replacing more than 8 million plastic bags. Each Morsbag is labeled with an iron-on patch with the project's web address printed on it, so the project self-perpetuates.

"Morsbags seems to leave no excuses," Claire says. "It is more than saying no to a plastic bag; it provides an immediate solution in the form of making something quick and easy that everybodyneeds with materials that most of the population already have on hand." The social aspect ismeaningful, too, as so many environmental projectsare important, but perhaps not all that fun. Morsbags, on the other hand, is great fun, creative, addictive, and a good way to meet local people and form communities.

"I'd like everyone to join in!" Claire says. "Some people say they have no time, but I know people who squeeze Morsbag-making into their extremely busy professional and personal lives. It's easy, fun, fab for whales, and is a finite project. If we all knuckled down and made a few Morsbags, we could end the plastic bag problem in months!"

To get involved, go to www.morsbags.com and register a pod. A pod can be composed of an individual or a group; all you need are a sewing machine, some space, and some material (the bag instructions are on the website). If you'd rather not set up a group yourself, then register on the forum and post a message in the "your area" section to let others know you are interested and how to reach you.

Natural Produce Bags

They are there, waiting for you, even in the most eco-friendly organic grocery stores: the single-use, plastic produce bag (cue the soundtrack from *Jaws*). Considering the time I spend carefully selecting the freshest organic fruits and vegetables, it seems a bit contradictory to then tuck them away in non-earth-friendly plastic bags. What's an eco-conscious food shopper to do? Whip up a few of these lightweight produce bags in organic cotton, and carry them along in the Denim Shopper (see page 104). They're a reusable, stylish, and biodegradable alternative to plastic, and they're perfect for bagging fruits, veggies, and even bulk food items such as nuts or cereal. To brighten up any routine shopping trip, add simple design elements from nature by making a few colorful leaf prints on your bags.

Materials

(Makes 4 bags)

1⅛ yards of 60"-wide organic cotton mesh,
   leno, gauze, or similar very lightweight,
   loosely woven cotton
4 yards of ½"-wide natural-color twill tape
Matching thread
Fabric shears
Disappearing-ink fabric marker
Safety pin
Fabric paint in olive, crimson, and amber
Foam paintbrush, 1" wide
Brayer or rolling pin
Paper towels
Waxed paper
Newspaper
Assortment of sturdy, pliable leaves
   in different shapes and sizes

PRINTING BY NATURE

In addition to leaves, you might also try printing with other natural elements, such as seed pods from maples or other trees or even slices of fruit.

Step 2
Cut rectangles.

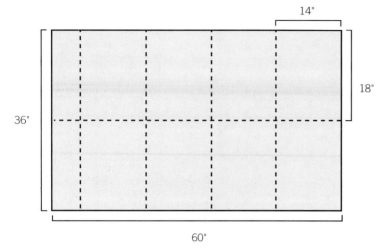

Step 5
Make drawstring casing.

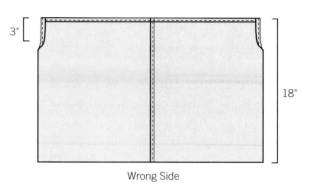

Wrong Side

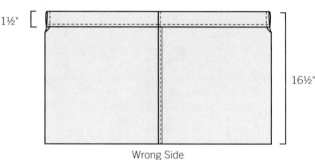

Wrong Side

❶ Prepare Fabric

Machine-wash and -dry the fabric, then iron it smooth.

❷ Cut Rectangles

Using a ruler and a disappearing-ink fabric marker, measure and mark two 14" x 18" rectangles of fabric for each bag. You will be able to cut out two rows of four rectangles across the width of the 60"-wide fabric, yielding eight rectangles (and four bags) total (see diagram above).

❸ Print Leaf Design

Lay newspaper on your work surface, and place a piece of scrap fabric (with either side facing up) on top of the newspaper. *Note: It is important to practice printing on scrap fabric before printing on the cut rectangles to ensure that you are producing the desired results.* Using a small amount

of paint and a foam brush, apply paint to the underside of a leaf. Place the leaf, paint side down, on top of the scrap fabric. Cover the leaf with a piece of paper towel, then a piece of waxed paper. Firmly press the leaf design into the fabric by rolling over the waxed paper with a brayer or rolling pin. Remove the waxed paper, paper towel, and leaf. Continue this process on your prepared rectangles, as desired.

After you have printed the fabric for each bag, let the paint dry completely, which requires at least a few hours. Then place the painted side of the fabric face down on a piece of white scrap paper. Cover your work with a scrap of fabric, and iron it on a low setting to heat-set the paint and make the fabric washable and colorfast.

❹ Begin Front-to-Back Assembly

With right sides together, layer, align, and pin one printed rectangle on top of one plain rectangle. Join the two rectangles by sewing a ¼" seam along one long (18") side. For durability, reinforce the seam: Press the seam's allowances to one side (see page 140), and, still working on the fabric's wrong side, topstitch the seam allowances ⅛" from the seam.

❺ Make Drawstring Casing

With the seamed rectangles opened out flat and wrong side up, fold and press the fabric's top edge ¼" to the wrong side; then edge-stitch (see page 133) the fold. Using a disappearing-ink fabric marker, mark 3" below the stitched top edge on each of the two un-sewn 18" sides of the rectangles. Fold and press the marked 3" of fabric on each top side edge ¼" to the wrong side, and edge-stitch these short folded edges (see diagram at top left). Finally fold down and press the top hem so that it meets the 3" marks at the sides, creating a 1½"-wide casing (see diagram at bottom left). Pin the folded edge evenly across the width of the sewn rectangles, and edge-stitch the casing's lower edge.

❻ Finish Bag

Align and pin the front and back rectangles, right sides together. Sew the remaining side and bottom edges together with a ¼" seam, starting just below the casing. Turn the bag right side out, and press it, covering any painted areas with a scrap of fabric to protect the iron. Edge-stitch the bottom seam and the remaining side seam ⅛" from the seams themselves to reinforce them, stitching one continuous line of stitches and backstitching (see page 133) at the beginning and end of your stitching.

❼ Add Drawstring

Cut 1 yard of ½"-wide twill tape, and pin a large safety pin at one end of the tape. Thread the pinned end of the tape through the opening at one end of the casing, and use the safety pin to work the tape through and out the opening at the other end. Remove the safety pin, and knot together the two ends of the twill tape.

❽ Add Produce

Now you're all set to do right by your fruits and veggies. Take these bags along on your next trip to the grocery store or farmer's market, and bring home your purchases with a clear conscience.

BYOB Water-Bottle Sling

The BYOB Water-Bottle Sling is a smart way to take your reusable water bottle with you and keep it insulated. Shown here are two versions to fit your style and needs: a single sling for going solo and a double one for when you've got kids or Fido with you and not enough hands!

Finished Measurements

Single-bottle sling
   (holds one bottle up to 20 ounces):
   5½" x 10", excluding strap
Double-bottle sling
   (holds two 16- to 20-ounce bottles):
   9" x 11", excluding strap

Materials

½ yard of 45"-wide solid-color woven cotton
   or linen *(for exterior)*
½ yard of 45"-wide printed woven cotton
   (for lining)
½ yard of 45"-wide fusible fleece or insulated
   batting
1⅙ yards (42") of 1"-wide nylon webbing
   (for single sling)
4" of 1" wide elastic
   (for double sling)
Thread in a coordinating color
Embroidery floss and embroidery needle
   (optional)
2 metal rings, 1½" in diameter
   (for single sling)
Fabric shears
Chalk fabric marker
4 to 6 safety pins

SINGLE SLING

❶ Prepare Fabric
Prewash and -dry all fabrics, except for the fleece/batting.

❷ Cut Out Sling Pieces
Lay the exterior fabric right side up and single layer, not folded. Using the patterns provided on page 107, cut out two Main Panels for each sling you're making (you'll need to move the pattern to cut the second piece). Next use the same Main Panel pattern to cut two Main Panels from the batting (if you're using fusible fleece, be sure that the fusible side of the fleece is facing up). Then lay the lining fabric flat and single layer, flip the Main Panel pattern over, and cut two identical lining pieces, moving the pattern to cut the second piece (the cut lining pieces will be the reverse of the cut exterior and batting pieces).

Finally, cut three Bottom pieces: two from the lining fabric, and one from the fleece/batting.

❸ Embroider Exterior Panel (optional)
If you want to add embroidery to the front of your sling, designate one exterior panel as the sling's front. Following the placement shown in drawing on page 107, mark the embroidery design on the right side of the fabric with a chalk fabric marker. Using embroidery floss and an embroidery needle, hand-embroider the design with backstitches (see page 134) and French knots (see page 135), as indicated on the pattern.

❹ Apply Fleece/Batting to Main Panels

Trim away the ¼" seam allowance from all sides of the fleece or batting main panels. If you are using fusible fleece, center the fleece pieces on the exterior main panels, with the fusible side of the fleece facing the wrong side of the exterior fabric. Cover the fleece and fabric with a press cloth, and iron the pair to fuse them together, following the fleece manufacturer's instructions.

If you are using a non-fusible batting, center the batting pieces on the wrong side of the exterior main panels, and temporarily secure the batting with safety pins, pinning from the right side of the exterior fabric and avoiding the panels' edges and any embroidery (in the next step, you'll topstitch the batting to secure it).

For the bottom piece, trim the seam allowance from the fleece/batting bottom, and secure it to the wrong side of one of the two lining-fabric bottoms by fusing it (if you're using fusible fleece) or with a safety pin (if you're using batting).

❺ Attach Lining to Sling Pieces

With the fabrics' right sides together, lay the front lining panel on top of the front exterior panel, and align and pin the edges. Sew all sides together with a ¼" seam, except for the bottom edge of the panel. Remove the pins, and clip the seam allowances (see page 140) along the curve and at the corners of the sewn panels, then turn the work right side out through the bottom opening. Use a chopstick to gently push out the corners from inside the work. Press the piece flat.

Edge-stitch (see page 133) all the seams from the right side, ⅛" from the edge. Then stitch straight across the unsewn bottom edge, ³⁄₁₆" from the edge, to secure the layers. Repeat the process for the back of the sling.

For the bottom panel, place the lining pieces wrong sides together and stitch around the perimeter with a ¼" seam. Do not trim or clip the seam allowances.

❻ Assemble Sling

Lay the front sling on the back sling, with the lining sides facing together. Align and pin the side seams, and edge-stitch them on top of the previous edge-stitching line, backstitching (see page 133) at the beginning and end of the seams to reinforce them.

Turn the sling wrong side out, and pin the edge of the bottom panel to the sling's bottom opening, with right sides together and distributing the fabric evenly. (Clip the raw edges of the sling, about ⅛" into the seam line, to help ease the fabric around the curve of the bottom.) Slowly stitch around the bottom with a ¼" seam. Zigzag-stitch the seam allowances together as a unit to finish the raw edges. Turn the sling right side out.

❼ Attach Strap

Put one of the sling's narrow ends through one of the metal rings, fold over 1" of the end towards the lining, and pin the folded end to secure it. Topstitch across this folded edge, backstitching at the beginning and end of the stitching line. *Note: If the ring seems to get in the way of your regular machine foot, try using a zipper foot on your machine instead.* Repeat the process for the other side.

Cut the webbing for the strap at your desired length (the sling shown on page 105 has a 42"-long strap). Using a lighted match, carefully melt the webbing's cut edge to prevent unraveling. When the strap end has cooled, put it through one of the metal rings, fold it back 1", and secure it with two rows of top-stitching about ¼" apart. Repeat the process with the other end of the webbing, making sure that the strap is not twisted.

BYOB WATER-BOTTLE SLING PATTERNS

Note: Lay fabric in a single layer to cut out patterns.

(Photocopy at 200%)

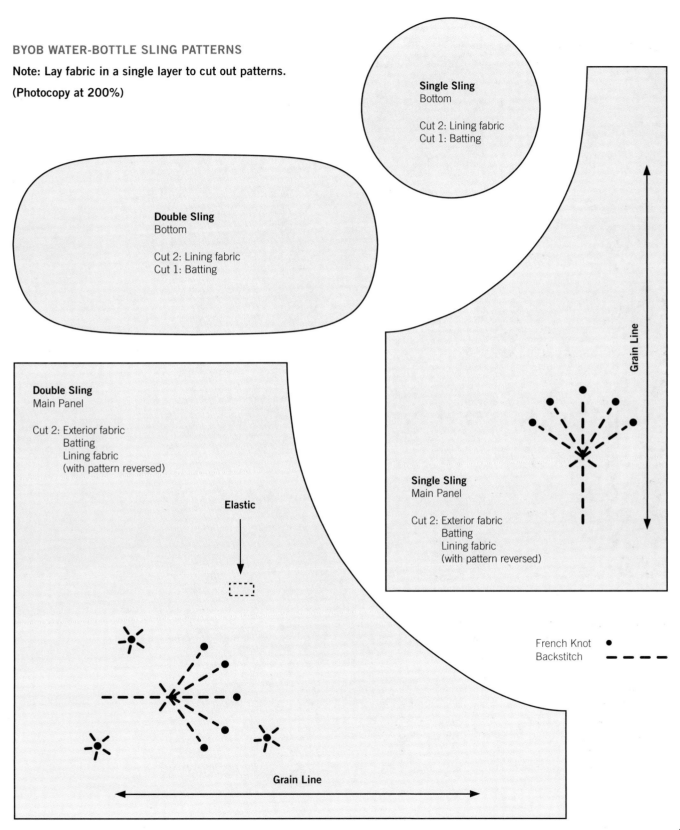

Single Sling
Bottom

Cut 2: Lining fabric
Cut 1: Batting

Double Sling
Bottom

Cut 2: Lining fabric
Cut 1: Batting

Grain Line

Double Sling
Main Panel

Cut 2: Exterior fabric
Batting
Lining fabric
(with pattern reversed)

Elastic

Single Sling
Main Panel

Cut 2: Exterior fabric
Batting
Lining fabric
(with pattern reversed)

French Knot ●
Backstitch – – – –

Grain Line

IT'S A WASH

Here are some tips to make every step of laundering and prepping
your new or used fabrics a little bit greener.

BETTER DETERGENT

Did you know that most commercial laundry
detergents contain petroleum-based oil and
potentially harmful chemicals? Replacing your
petroleum-based detergent with a vegetable-based
one is better for your health (no toxic chemicals),
and for the earth (biodegradable), and decreases
our oil dependency. According to Seventh Generation, an eco-friendly household-products company
(seventhgeneration.com), if every home in
the United States replaced just one 100-ounce
bottle of petroleum-based liquid laundry detergent
with one 100-ounce bottle of a vegetable-based
product, we could save 460,000 barrels of oil.
There are many eco-friendly detergents on the
market, such as those made by Ecover, Mrs.
Meyers Clean Day, and Seventh Generation.
You can also make your own detergent. The
recipe below is from Sandy Shields of
thefrugalshopper.com.

BAKING SODA

Add ½ cup baking soda to rinse cycle of washing
machine to deodorize, soften, and freshen laundry.
To remove yellow stains and to brighten old linens,
add 4 tablespoons baking soda to wash cycle.

CLOTHESLINE

According to consumerenergycenter.org, if you
consistently air-dry laundry instead of using a
machine dryer, over time you will reduce your
energy bill by 5 to 10 percent.

PRESSING

Use an iron with an energy-saving auto shut-off
feature. If the iron is left undisturbed for several
minutes, it will shut off to save energy and
prevent fires.

Powdered Laundry Detergent

All of these ingredients are
generally sold in the bar-soap
or laundry-detergent aisle of
well-stocked supermarkets.

1 cup grated Fels Naptha
   or Ivory soap
½ cup washing soda
   (not the same as baking soda)
½ cup borax

Combine the three ingredients,
and store in a well-sealed
container. For a light load,
use 1 tablespoon. For a big
or heavily-soiled load, use
2 tablespoons.

DOUBLE SLING

❶ Prepare Fabric

Follow Step 1 for the Single Sling on page 104.

❷ Cut Out Sling Pieces

Follow Step 2 for the Single Sling, then cut one 2" x 36" strip from each of the exterior and lining fabrics for a strap.

❸ Embroider Exterior Panel (optional) and Apply Fleece/Batting

Follow steps 3 and 4 for the Single Sling.

❹ Seam Strap to Back Panel

With the fabrics' right sides together, align one end of the strap lining with the narrow end of the back-panel lining. Pin and join the ends together with a ¼" seam, and then press the seam allowances open (see page 140). Repeat this process to join the exterior-fabric strap and exterior-fabric back panel.

❺ Attach Lining to Sling Pieces

With the fabrics' right sides together, lay the front lining panel on top of the front exterior panel, and align and pin the edges together. Join all sides with a ¼" seam, except for the narrow top edge and the bottom edge. Remove the pins, and clip the seam allowances along the curve and at the corner, then turn the work right side out through the bottom opening. Use a chopstick to gently push out the corners from inside the work. Press the piece flat.

Edge-stitch all seams from the right side. Also straight-stitch across the unsewn bottom edge, 3⁄16" from the edge, to secure the layers. Leave the narrow end unsewn.

Repeat the process for the back panel, this time sewing all sides and the length of the strap but leaving the strap end and the back panel's bottom edge open. Remove the pins, and clip the seam allowances along the curve and at the corners; then turn the work right side out through the bottom opening. (To help turn the strap right side out, secure the strap end with a safety pin, and push the pinned end down inside the strap and work it towards the main part of the sling.) Use a

chopstick to gently push out the corner by inserting it inside the work. Press the piece flat. Edge-stitch all seams from the right and work it towards the main part of the sling.) Use a chopstick to gently push out the corner by inserting it inside the work. Press the piece flat. Edge-stitch all seams from the right side. Also seam the bottom edge (which was not previously sewn and turned), 3⁄16" from the edge, to secure the layers. Leave the strap end unsewn. For the bottom panel, place the lining pieces wrong sides together. Stitch around the perimeter of the bottom panel with ¼" seam. Do not trim or snip the seam allowances.

❻ Assemble Sling

Follow Step 6 for the Single Sling.

❼ Attach Strap

At the opening of the narrow top edge of the front sling, fold ¼" of the raw edges (of both the exterior and lining fabrics) to the wrong side, that is, down into the center of the narrow top edge, and press the folded edges. Insert ½" of the loose end of the strap into the opening, making sure that the strap is not twisted. Topstitch the strap in place, securing all layers and backstitching at the beginning and end of the stitching line.

❽ Attach Elastic Divider

To keep the bottles in place and provide flexibility in terms of bottle size, attach a small elastic divider inside the sling. Fold each end of the 4" length of 1"-wide elastic back on itself by ½". Stitch across each end to hem it, backstitching at the beginning and end of the stitching line to secure it.

Following the placement mark indicated on the pattern, pin one end of the elastic to the inside of the pouch (that is, the lining). Keeping the strap and other parts of the sling free of the needle, carefully stitch the elastic end in place by stitching a rectangle around its ½" hemmed area. Flip the bag over, and pin the elastic's other hemmed edge to the lining of the sling's other side, following the pattern's placement marking. It may help you to hand-baste this end in place before stitching by taking a few long stitches with a hand-needle and thread. Finally, machine-stitch this end as you did the first end. Remove any hand-basted stitches.

❾ Reuse, Refresh

Tuck an eco-friendly reusable water bottle in your sling and be on your way.

Auto Sunshade

One way that global warming really burns me up is when I have to sit on a hot car seat. Ouch! Using a reflective sunshade in your windshield can reduce heat while preventing interior sun damage to your vehicle. This sunshade design uses empty Mylar juice pouches—otherwise non-recyclable items—to reflect intense sun rays, keeping your car cool so that you don't have to rely so heavily on the A/C.

You'll find it's disturbingly easy to collect a boatload of drink pouches after nearly any Saturday afternoon kids' soccer game, since this drink (and packaging) has become a standard offering. Also, keep an eye out for them at birthday parties, Scout meetings, and at the community pool.

Finished Measurements

30" high x 45" wide (or, with optional extra panel added, 53" wide)

Materials

Empty Mylar drink pouches, such as Capri Sun or Kool-Aid Juicers: 86 for 45"-wide shade; 100 for 53"-wide shade (counts includes 2 extra pouches for testing)

6 yards of extra-wide (½") double-fold bias tape in any color

Scissors

Tape measure

Heavy-duty, jeans machine-needle

Large paper clips, about 6

PREP WORK

This project is not for the delicate sewer or sewing machine: As with most large projects using bulky materials, there will be a bit of wrestling involved, especially when you near the end of the assembly. The key is to give yourself plenty of room by clearing off your sewing table so that it holds only the project and your machine. Be sure that your machine is in good working order and can handle sewing heavier materials (if you're unsure, try sewing one pouch to see how your machine behaves). Sew slowly and take your time—those juice pouches aren't going anywhere!

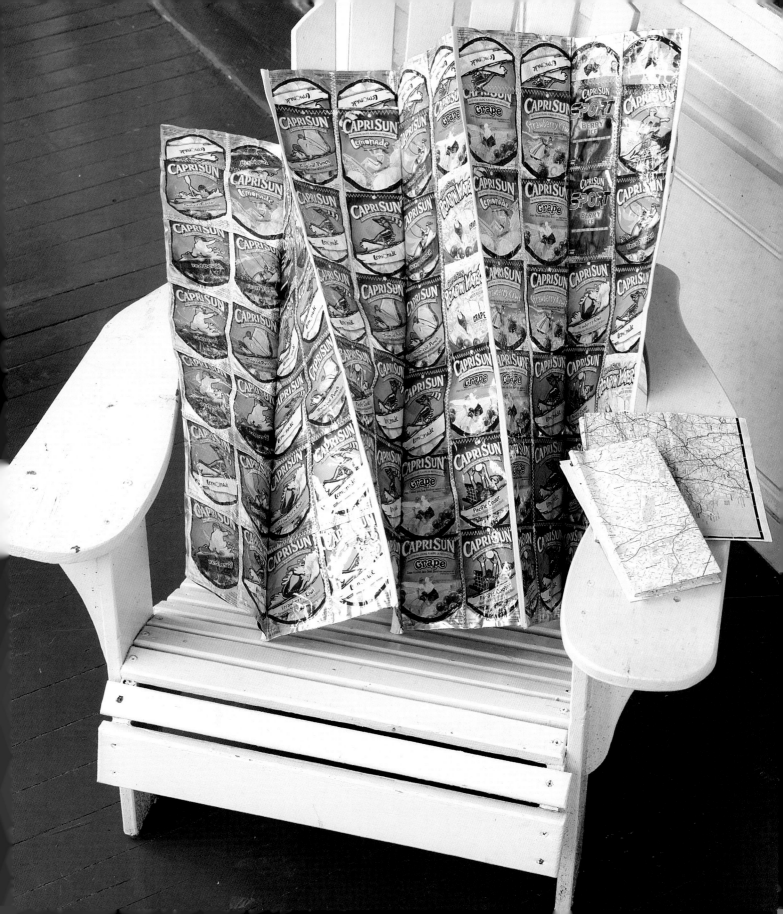

Steps 5 and 6
Sew pouches into strips,
then sew strips into panels.

Single Strip   Double-Strip Panel

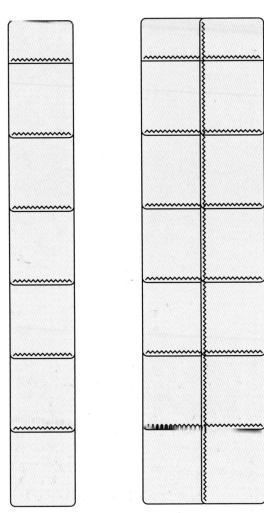

❶ Prepare Materials

As you collect used juice pouches, trim ¼" off the top edge above the opening for the straw. Discard the straw and trimmed piece. Open the top of the pouch, rinse the pouch with warm, soapy water, and air-dry it.

❷ Measure Windshield

Take all measurements from inside the windshield: Using a tape measure, measure the width of the windshield along the top edge. Next take the measurement from the windshield's center top edge to its center bottom edge, where the windshield meets the dash.

❸ Plan Your Shade

The 45"-wide sunshade consists of six vertical panels of pouches, with each panel made of two strips of sewn pouches equaling about 30" in height and 8" in width. If your wind-shield is wider than 45", you'll need to make one extra panel (which requires collecting about 14 extra pouches) for a total of seven panels and a finished width of 53". To change the sunshade's height, add to or subtract from the number of pouches used in each panel.

❹ Set Up Machine

Before doing any stitching, it's wise to practice sewing on a Mylar pouch to get the correct machine tension: First, install a heavy-duty jeans needle in your machine, and set the machine for a wide zigzag stitch with a stitch length of about 2.5. Then zigzag-stitch a few inches on an extra juice pouch, and stop to check your stitches. They should not appear to pull too tightly or sit too loosely on top of the Mylar. You may need to experiment with loosening or tightening the upper tension on your machine to produce even stitches that look the same on the top and bottom of the fabric (see your machine manual if you're unsure of how to adjust the upper tension). Remember to sew slowly and to replace a needle if it gets bent or otherwise damaged while you're sewing.

❺ Sew Pouches Into Strips

To begin, you'll assemble individual pouches into long strips equaling the height of your windshield. (Keep in mind that the pouches' juice logos should all be turned to one side of the work and their silver sides to the other.) To assemble each long strip, start by overlapping the bottom edge of one pouch ¼" over the top edge of a second pouch. Secure the overlapped edges with paper clips (since Mylar is difficult to pin through), and zigzag-stitch the pouches together

across the overlap. Overlap the bottom edge of a third pouch ¼" over the top edge of the two joined pouches, and paper-clip and sew the two edges as above. Continue adding and sewing pouches to the top of the strip until the strip is at least six pouches long; then stop to measure it. Depending on the way the pouches were trimmed and overlapped, you will probably need to add one more pouch (for a total of seven pouches per strip) to get the full length you need. This last pouch may need to be trimmed down to produce your desired length.

In order to get a clean, finished look for the edge of the sunshade, when you sew on the last pouch at the top of the strip, turn the last pouch around so that its curved bottom edge serves as the end of the strip (see the drawing at left). Create 11 more strips for the 45"-wide shade (or 13 more for the 53"-wide shade), repeating the steps above.

❻ Sew Strips Into Panels

Place two strips with their logo sides facing up. Overlap the long edge of one strip over the other by ¼". Since you can't paper-clip these long edges together, keep an eye on them to make sure the ¼" overlap is consistent as you slowly zigzag-stitch the overlapped edges to create one double-strip panel. Don't worry if the individual pouch seams on the two strips don't match up exactly. The important thing is that all of the panels are the same length. Depending on the overall width of your windshield, you'll need to make about six or seven double-strip panels.

❼ Assemble Shade

Once your panels are completed, you'll join them with bias tape (see page 136 for more information on working with bias tape). *Note: If you are new to using bias tape, you might want to practice this step on an extra juice pouch before you begin assembling the shade.*

> **"**I only feel angry when I see waste. When I see people throwing away things we could use.**"**
>
> **MOTHER TERESA**

Step 7
Assemble shade with bias tape

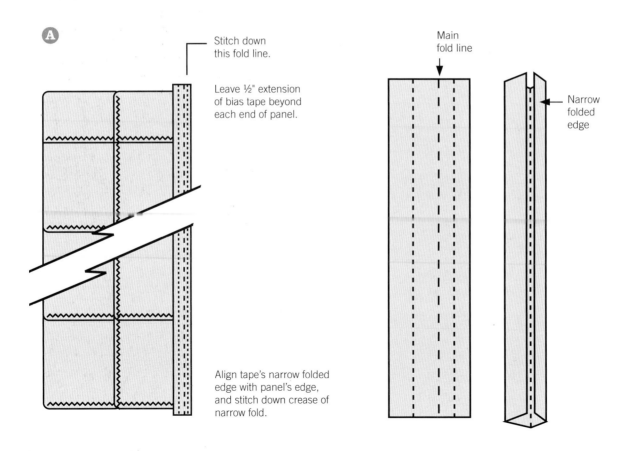

A

Stitch down this fold line.

Leave ½" extension of bias tape beyond each end of panel.

Align tape's narrow folded edge with panel's edge, and stitch down crease of narrow fold.

Main fold line

Narrow folded edge

B

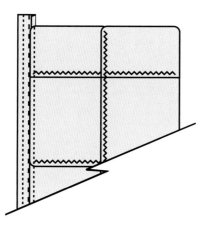

Turn panel over.

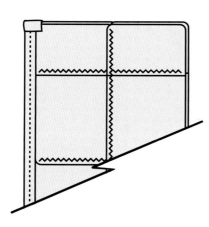

Place second panel on top of first, and fold down ½" bias-tape extensions.

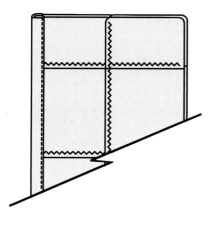

Fold length of tape around panels' edges, enclosing them, and edge-stitch tape.

A: Set one panel, logo side up, on a flat surface. Cut a length of double-fold bias tape that equals the panel's height plus 1". Open up the tape's folds, and align and paper-clip the tape's narrow folded edge with the long edge of the Mylar panel, allowing ½" of bias tape to extend past the panel's top and bottom edges (see the drawings at left). Straight-stitch along the crease of the tape's narrow fold (about ¼" from the edge).

B: Turn the panel over. Place a second panel on top of the first, logo side up, so that the panels' silver sides face together. Fold down the ½" bias-tape extensions at the panels' top and bottom edges, then fold the length of the bias tape up and over both panels' edges, enclosing these edges. Secure the taped edges with paper clips. Then slowly and carefully edge-stitch (see page 133) the binding's edge through all layers (see the drawing at left).

C: Repeat these steps, this time applying the instructions in A to the edge of the silver side of the second panel. Then place a third panel on top of the second, silver side up and logo sides together, repeating the directions in B. Continue this process, alternating the binding from the silver side to the logo side of the panels and creating an accordion pleating pattern (see the drawing below) until you've assembled all your panels.

❽ Chill Out

Next time you park your car, you'll be made in the shade! Simply unfold the sunshade, and place it in your windshield with the silver side facing out. Flip the car's visors down to hold the sunshade in place. Your car will stay noticeably cooler on hot sunny days. And when you're ready to go, your shade's accordion design folds flat for easy storage. Now you're recycling and beating the heat. You are so cool!

C Accordian pleating pattern with binding

Picnic Blanket

Picnics are a relaxing way to get out and enjoy the fresh air. Create a dry, comfortable spot for your adventure by repurposing a vinyl tablecloth and a few soft terry-cloth towels (a variation of the tried-and-true "sit-upon" mats I remember making in my Girl Scout days).

Materials

1 round vinyl tablecloth, 60" in diameter
5 or 6 large terry-cloth bath towels,
    in complementary colors
5 yards of ball-fringe trim, in accent color
Fabric shears
Paper scissors
Shelf paper or brown wrapping paper,
    at least 40" square *(for making patterns)*

❶ Prepare Materials
Machine-wash and -dry all the towels before starting your project.

❷ Make Your Pattern
Open the tablecloth on a large surface like the floor. Fold the tablecloth in half, then into quarters, and finally into eighths. Trace this pie shape on your large piece of paper, and cut out the traced pattern with paper scissors.

tip

CHOOSING TOWELS AND TABLECLOTHS

- Used terry-cloth towels and vinyl tablecloths can usually be found at thrift stores or in your own linen closet. Look for towels without fading, snags, or holes.

- Vinyl tablecloths should be in near-new condition. Better yet, you may find an unused tablecloth at a resale shop still in its original package.

- Let the design of the tablecloth guide you when choosing towel colors. For further embellishment, you might want to create an appliqué based on a motif from the tablecloth to sew onto the terry-cloth side of the blanket.

❸ Cut Pie Shapes

Lay one towel on a large cutting surface. Place the pattern piece lengthwise on the towel. Avoid using any part of the towel that does not lie flat (some towels have decorative woven bands near the ends that may cause puckering). Pin the pattern to the towel, and cut out the shape using fabric shears.

To create interest in your design, vary the size of the pie shape. To make narrower wedges, which are good for using up narrow scraps of towel, fold the pattern piece lengthwise, making sure to maintain the full length of the original wedge shape regardless of the new angle. To make wider wedges, create a wider pattern piece by beginning to fold the tablecloth as you did in Step 2 but not folding it into eighths (be sure, though, not to make the pattern's curve wider than the widest towel you're working with). As you cut more shapes out of each towel, arrange them on the tablecloth.

❹ Assemble Shapes

Once you have enough shapes to cover the tablecloth, arrange them in your desired composition, varying the size and color of the pieces. Set your sewing machine on a wide zigzag stitch with a stitch length of 2-3. Sew two adjacent pie shapes together by butting the edges of the pieces and zigzag-stitching the butted edges, starting at the points and working toward the curved edge. Take the next pie shape and join it to the first two, again butting and zigzag-stitching the edges together as before. Continue this process until you have assembled the entire circle. Don't worry if your points are wobbly or not perfectly matched. In the next step, you will add a center for reinforcement that will hide any less-than-perfect points.

❺ Add Center

Using a plate or lid as a template, trace a large circle (6" to 8" in diameter) on a piece of paper, and cut out the traced shape with paper scissors. Pin the paper pattern to a towel scrap, and cut out the circle with fabric shears. Smooth out the assembled blanket front, and place and pin the new circle directly over the center intersection of all the pie shapes. Zigzag-stitch around the edge of the center circle, attaching it to the blanket front.

❻ Embellish Tablecloth

With the wrong side (back) of the tablecloth facing up, pin the braided edge of the ball fringe to the edge of the tablecloth, allowing the balls to dangle over the edge of the tablecloth. Using a medium zigzag stitch, sew down the center of the braid around the entire perimeter.

❼ Sew Front to Back

This next step is best done on a smooth work surface (not on carpeting!). With the right side of the tablecloth facing up, mark the center with a safety pin (you can find the center by first folding the tablecloth in quarters; the "point" is the center). Then turn the tablecloth right side down. Lay the terry-cloth blanket front on top of the tablecloth, right side up. Mark the center of the blanket front with a safety pin. By reaching between the layers, feel for the pin on both layers to be sure the centers are aligned. Once they are, pin through both layers. Using the palm of your hands, smooth out the terry cloth by moving from the center to the outer edge of the circle. Pin the layers together around the perimeter. If the blanket front extends beyond the tablecloth, you can trim it off after sewing the layers together. Using a medium zigzag-stitch and making sure that the braid of the ball fringe is sandwiched between the two layers, sew the tablecloth's front and back together around the perimeter, backstitching (see page 133) at the beginning and end of the seam.

❽ Pack It Up

Now that your picnic blanket is done, it's time to head for the great outdoors. To fold your blanket, grab the sides, and fold them to the center as you would fold a burrito. Then fold and roll from one end to the other. You'll be ready for a spontaneous outing with nothing to dampen your spirits, or your picnic.

REDUCING TEXTILE WASTE

Where do socks go? I'm not refering to the pair separated on laundry day. I mean old worn-out socks, plus T-shirts, curtains, towels, and the like. The average American throws away about 68 pounds of textiles every year, comprising up to 4.5 percent of the space in our landfills (according to the Environmental Protection Agency). Although 2.5 billion pounds of textile waste is recycled annually (reclaimed as secondhand clothing, turned into wiping and polishing cloths, or converted into fiber to be used in new textiles), the Council for Textile Recycling estimates that this represents only 20 percent of all textile waste.

Here are a few ways you can help to keep textile waste out of our landfills:

Reduce consumption. You may think you need new linens or that new dress, but sometimes less really is more.

Reuse and repurpose. Use your craftiness to refashion your used textiles. For instance, old pillowcases can be made into the simple skirt on page 124, and out-of-fashion sweaters can be felted and sewn into cozy slippers (page 48). If a textile is too worn to refashion into clothing, reuse it as a rag or a polishing cloth.

Buy secondhand. Thrift and consignment shops are often full of nearly-new items at affordable prices. Visit thethriftshopper.com, a national thrift store directory, to find a charity-driven thrift store in your area.

Swap, donate, or hand it down. Start a clothing swap in your neighborhood. Donate clothing to a charity, such as Goodwill or the Salvation Army. Check out freecycle.org, a nonprofit movement of people who are giving (and getting) stuff free in their own towns. Got kids? Join freepeats.org to find or pass on gently-used baby, kid, and maternity clothing, and more.

Quality clothing. When you do choose new, purchase clothing and textile products that are high quality and designed to last.

Make this your mantra. "Use it up. Wear it out. Make it do. Do without." (This saying was popularized during the World War II rationing efforts.)

Beach Bag

From tabletop accent to poolside tote, this funky set of Marimekko placemats can quickly be transformed into a stylish beach bag. Since most placemats already have a lining, you're halfway done before you've even begun!

Finished Measurements
About 16" wide x 12" high x 6" deep

Materials
Set of 4 placemats
   (I used 16½" x 12½" placemats)
3 to 4 yards of 1¼"-wide cotton webbing
   *(for straps; length depends on
   placemat size)*
Fabric shears
Ruler or measuring tape
Disappearing-ink fabric marker

CHOOSING PLACEMATS

Choose placemats that are lined and feel sturdy enough to function as a dependable tote bag. Since the bag will likely hold wet bathing suits and towels, consider waterproofing the placemats with a nontoxic waterproofing product such as Nikwax (see Resources on page 141) before sewing them together.

❶ **Cut Tote Bottom**
Designate one placemat as the Tote Front and another as the Tote Back, and set the pair aside. Use the third placemat to make the Tote Bottom: Measure one of the placemat's short sides, and divide the measurement in half to find the midpoint of this side (mine was 6¼"). Mark this point with a disappearing-ink fabric marker, and make a corresponding mark on the other short side. Using a ruler, draw a line between the marked points. Use fabric shears to cut the placemat in half along this line. One half will become the Tote Bottom; the other half is scrap. Finish the raw, cut edge of the Tote Bottom with a wide zigzag stitch.

Steps 1 and 2
Use placemats as shown below to create Tote Front, Back, Bottom, and Sides.

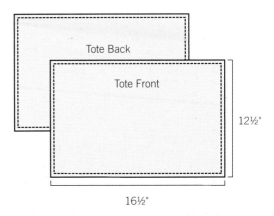

Tote Back

Tote Front

12½"

16½"

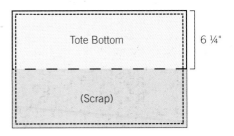

Tote Bottom

6 ¼"

(Scrap)

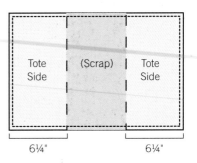

Tote Side

(Scrap)

Tote Side

6¼"

6¼"

❷ Cut Tote Sides

Use the fourth placemat to make the Tote Sides: The length of the short side of the Tote Bottom determines the width of the Tote Side (mine was 6¼"). Starting from the short end of the fourth placemat, mark this measurement along one long side of the placemat with the disappearing-ink fabric marker; then measure and mark the other long side, starting from the same short end. Using a ruler, draw a line connecting these points. Cut along this line to create one Tote Side.

Repeat the measuring, marking, and cutting from the other short end of the fourth placemat to create the second Tote Side. Finish the cut edges of the Tote Sides with a wide zigzag stitch. *Note: Most placemats have a row of topstitching around the perimeter, about ¼" from the edge. You can use this as a handy guide to stitch along as you assemble your bag.*

❸ Sew Front, Back, and Bottom

Begin working with the placemat designated as the Tote Front and the rectangle created as the Tote Bottom: With the right sides of these rectangles facing up, match up their long sides. Then overlap the Tote Front edge over the Tote Bottom edge by ½", and pin the overlapped edges to secure them. Straight-stitch the overlapped edges together, creating a lapped seam (see page 139) and backstitching (see page 133) at the beginning and end of the seam to secure the stitches. Repeat this process with the Tote Back, overlapping the Tote Back's long edge over the Tote Bottom's long edge, stitching a ½" lapped seam to join the two edges, and backstitching at the beginning and end of the seam to secure it.

❹ Lay Out Straps

Lay the attached Tote Front/Bottom/Back on your work surface, right side up. Following the diagram at right, lay out the cotton webbing in a long oval shape to create the bag's straps, starting and stopping near the center of the Tote Bottom. Be sure that the straps are the same length (20" is a good length for carrying over the shoulder) and spaced 5" apart across the center of the pieces. Pin the straps in place on the Tote Front/Bottom/Back, and zigzag-stitch across the ends of the webbing where the straps meet on the Tote Bottom panel.

Steps 4 and 5
Lay out and stitch straps.

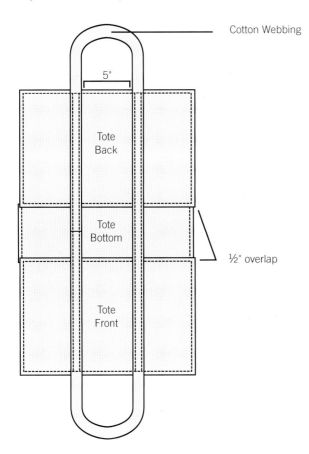

Cotton Webbing

5"

Tote Back

Tote Bottom

Tote Front

½" overlap

❺ Stitch Straps

Starting at the top edge of the Tote Front, edge-stitch (see page 133) down one side of the webbing, across the Tote Bottom and the Tote Back. When you reach the top edge of the Tote Back, stop with the needle down, and pivot (see page 140) the work so that you can stitch across the webbing. When you reach the other side of the webbing, stop again, with the needle down, and pivot the work, so that you can continue edge-stitching back down the webbing's other edge; and stitch over the first ½" or so of your beginning stitches to secure them. Repeat this process to edge-stitch the second side of the webbing.

❻ Attach Sides

With the right sides facing up, align one long edge of one Tote Side with the short edge of the Tote Front. Then overlap the Tote Front ½" over the Tote Side, and pin the overlapped edges in place. Straight-stitch the edges together, creating a lapped seam and stopping ½" from the corner. Remove the tote from the machine.

Next overlap the short edge of the Tote Bottom ½" over the short edge of the Tote Side, and pin the overlapped edges in place. Straight-stitch the pair together, creating a lapped seam and stopping ½" from the corner. Remove the tote from the machine.

Starting at the top edge of the Tote Back, overlap the short edge of Tote Back ½" over the long edge of the Tote Side, and pin the overlapped edges in place. Straight-stitch the edges together into the corner, creating a lapped seam. Repeat this process to attach the other Tote Side.

❼ Throw in the Towel

Grab your shades and pack up your new tote. It's time to head for the beach.

Easy, Breezy Skirt

This quick skirt is a cheerful pick-me-up for any wardrobe. Refashioned from a pillowcase with only a few notions, in no time (really—less than an hour!), you'll have a cool summertime skirt ready to wear.

Finished Measurements

Small/Medium *(size shown)*: Waist, 30";
   hip, 40"; length, 23"
   (For information on larger sizes, see the note
   in the Materials list below.)

Materials

1 standard-size cotton percale pillowcase
   *Note: Most pillowcases are about 20" wide
   (or a total of 40" in circumference) and will
   yield enough fabric for a woman's size Small
   to Medium skirt. For larger sizes, or if you
   want to make this skirt with yardage or a bed
   sheet rather than with a pillowcase, you'll
   need about 1 yard of a lightweight woven
   fabric, such as cotton calico or broadcloth.*
1 yard of ¾"-wide elastic
1¼ yards of ribbon or other decorative trim
   (optional; I used 1"-wide rickrack)
Coordinating thread
Fabric shears
Disappearing-ink fabric marker
Large safety pin

tip

PILLOWCASE POINTERS

If you're using a pillowcase to make your skirt, take advantage of its existing details: Use the hemmed opening as the hem of the skirt. And if your pillowcase features a border print, embroidered edging, or even a ruffle, it can become a design element along the skirt's hem. Look for unique pillowcases in the linens department of your local thrift shop or in your own closets. A skirt made from a vintage pillowcase will give you a retro look cheap!

❶ Prepare Materials

Launder and press the pillowcase or fabric, and lay the pillowcase/fabric flat and right side up on your work surface. If you're working with a pillowcase, go to Step 2. If you're working with yardage, skip to Step 3.

❷ Measure and Cut Pillowcase

Using fabric shears, cut open the seamed short end of the pillowcase opposite the opening. To establish your desired length, try on the skirt if you're making it for yourself, or have its intended wearer try it on: Step into the pillowcase—the hemmed opening will become the bottom of the skirt and the cut opening its waist—and position the hem where you want the skirt's finished length to fall. Fold over the excess fabric at the waist, and mark the waist at the fold with the disappearing-ink fabric marker.

Take off the pillowcase, and lay it flat on your work surface. Draw a line from side seam to side seam at the waistline mark using the disappearing-ink fabric marker. *Note: If your pillowcase has only one side seam—and many pillowcases do—mark the fold opposite the seam, and treat it as a side seam.* Measure and mark a second line 1¼" above the first for the waistband casing. Using fabric shears, cut along the second (top) line. Then proceed to Step 4.

❸ Measure and Cut Fabric

If you're working with yardage, measure the widest part of your hip and add 3" to determine the width you'll need. Then measure from the waist to your desired skirt length, and add 4½" to determine the needed length. Cut a rectangle of fabric to these dimensions.

Fold the cut fabric rectangle in half widthwise, with right sides together, and sew a ½" side seam along the aligned, long raw edges, creating a fabric tube. Zigzag-stitch the seam allowances together as a unit to finish them. Fold and press the bottom edge of the tube ¼" to the wrong side. Fold, press, and pin the hem up another 3". Then edge-stitch (see page 133) the folded hem, stitching over the beginning stitches by about ½" to anchor them when you arrive back where you began stitching.

❹ Make Waistband Casing

To finish the top edge of the skirt, fold the fabric ¼" to the wrong side, and press and edge-stitch the edge. Fold the top edge 1" more to the wrong side, and pin it in place. Then stitch ⅞" from the top fold to create the waistband casing, leaving a 2" opening at the side seam.

Attach a safety pin to one end of the cut elastic, insert the elastic's pinned end in the casing's opening, and work the elastic through and out the other end of the opening, taking care not to twist it in the casing. Overlap the elastic ends, and secure them with the safety pin. Try on the skirt again, and pull the elastic through the 2" opening to adjust it to your desired fit, re-pinning the elastic's overlapped ends to secure any adjustment you make.

❺ Sew Elastic and Close Casing

Remove the skirt, pull the pinned ends of the elastic out of the casing opening, and stitch across the elastic's overlapped ends next to the safety pin; then sew back across the elastic in reverse to secure it. Remove the safety pin, trim off any excess length on the elastic ends, and push the elastic back into the casing. Finally topstitch the casing's opening to close it.

❻ Add Decorative Trim (optional)

Depending on your style and that of the original pillowcase, you might want to embellish your skirt with ribbon, rickrack, or other trim. Most pillowcases have a wide hem at the opening, and my favorite place to add trim is along this line of hem stitching. To do this, pin the trim along the stitching line, beginning at the side seam; and then, for a clean finish, tuck under and pin the trim's second raw end when you arrive back at your starting point. Straight-stitch the trim in place all the way around the circumference of the hem, stitching down the center of the trim if it's narrow (or top-stitching along each edge if the trim is wider) and ending at the side seam where you began. Backstitch (see page 133) the beginning and end of your stitching to secure the stitches.

❼ Kick Back

This skirt sews up fast, so you'll have plenty of free time on your hands to enjoy wearing it. Put it on, admire your work, and take it easy.

FEEDSACK COUTURE

In the late 1800s, plain cotton feedsacks were used to package bulk goods, such as flour, sugar, and animal feed. Thrifty farm wives quickly discovered that these cotton bags yielded utilitarian fabric to be used for dishcloths, diapers, nightgowns, and other household textiles. And manufacturers quickly realized that they could use desirable printed sacks as a marketing ploy to build brand loyalty. A dress, for example, might take several identical sacks to create, and so the farmer might be inclined to purchase more to ensure that his wife would have enough fabric. Vintage feedsacks remain collectible today as the popularity of retro prints and patterns continue to inspire everyone from the DIY sewer to textile and fashion designers.

Girl's Easy, Breezy Sundress

This cheerful summer dress makes creative use of a colorful pillowcase, adopting its hemmed opening as the hem of the dress. The design's simple styling and adjustable ties will accommodate a growing girl for summers to come. Add a little trim here and there—or incorporate the existing details of your pillowcase, such as a border print, embroidered edging, or ruffle at the opening's hem—and you've got a cheerful frock any little girl would love to wear.

Finished Measurements

12M: Width at hem, 20";
   length, neck to hem, 16¾"
18M: Width at hem, 20";
   length, neck to hem, 17½"
2T: Width at hem, 20";
   length, neck to hem, 18¼"
3T: Width at hem, 20";
   length, neck to hem, 19" *(garment shown)*
4T: Width at hem, 20";
   length, neck to hem, 19¾"

Materials

1 standard-size cotton percale pillowcase, made from a print or embellished fabric
Note: If you want to use yardage or a bed sheet rather than a pillowcase, you'll need about ¾ yard of a lightweight woven fabric, such as cotton calico or broadcloth.
1 package extra-wide (½") double-fold bias tape in coordinating color
2 yards of ⅝"-wide ribbon, cut into two equal lengths
1¼ yards of jumbo rickrack or other decorative trim (optional)
Thread coordinating with pillowcase *(and with optional trim)*
Fabric shears
Disappearing-ink fabric marker
Safety pin

ARMHOLE PATTERN

All Sizes: 12M-4T

(Photocopy at 200%)

Align curve's top edge with top cut edge of pillowcase/sewn fabric.

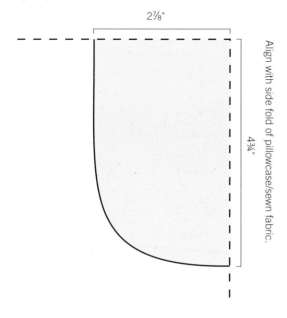

2⅞"

Align with side fold of pillowcase/sewn fabric.

4¾"

Cut positioned armhole curve through both fabric layers. Flip and reposition curve on fabric's other top edge to cut second armhole.

❶ Prepare Materials

Launder and press the pillowcase or yardage, if needed. Lay the pillowcase/fabric flat on your work surface. If you're working with a pillowcase, go to Step 2. If you're working with yardage, skip to Step 3.

❷ Measure and Cut Pillowcase

Measure the pillowcase starting from the hem, and mark the length according to your desired size: 12M = 18", 18M = 18 ¾", 2T = 19½", 3T = 20¼", 4T = 21". Using a disappearing-ink fabric marker, draw a line from side seam to side seam at your desired length (if your pillowcase has only one side seam—and many do—mark the fold opposite the side seam, and treat it as a second side seam). Using fabric shears, cut along the marked length line, removing any excess length. Proceed to Step 4.

❸ Measure and Cut Fabric

Measure and cut a rectangle from your fabric that's 41" wide by the length of your desired size (12M = 20¼", 18M = 21", 2T = 21¾", 3T = 22½", 4T = 23¼"). Fold the rectangle in half widthwise, with right sides together, and sew a ½" side seam along the aligned, long raw edges, creating a tube. Fold and press the bottom edge of the tube ¼" to the wrong side, and edge-stitch (see page 133) the fold. Then fold, press, and pin the bottom edge up another 2" to the wrong side; and edge-stitch the hem's upper fold.

❹ Cut Armholes

Using the armhole pattern provided at left, align the pattern with the fabric's top (cut) edge and its side seam. Pin through both layers of fabric, and cut out the armhole shape with fabric shears. Flip the pattern over and repeat the process, aligning the pattern with the top edge and the other side seam (or side fold) to cut the second armhole.

❺ Bind Armholes

Cut two 14" lengths of extra-wide double-fold bias tape, and bind each armhole with one length, following the instructions on page 137 for binding an edge with bias tape.

❻ Make Casings

To finish the top edge of the dress, fold and press the fabric on the front of the dress ¼" to the wrong side, and edge-stitch the folded edge. Fold, press, and pin this edge another 1" to the wrong side, and edge-stitch this new fold to create a casing.

Attach a safety pin to one end of 1 yard of ribbon, and work the ribbon through and out of the casing. Then cut the ends of the ribbon ties at a 45-degree angle to prevent fraying.

Repeat the process to create a casing across the top back edge of the dress.

❼ Add Decorative Trim (optional)

Depending on the recipient's style and that of the original pillowcase, you might want to embellish the dress with ribbon, rickrack, or another trim. Most pillowcases have a wide hem at the opening, and my favorite place to add trim is along this line of hem stitching. To do this, pin the trim along the stitching line, beginning at the side seam; and then, for a clean finish, tuck under and pin the trim's second raw end when you arrive back at your starting point. Straight-stitch down the center of the rickrack or other narrow trim (or stitch along the top and bottom edges of a wider trim) all the way around the circumference of the hem, ending at the side seam where you began. To secure the stitching, backstitch (see page 133) at the beginning and end of your stitching.

❽ Case Closed

Now that you're finished, you can dress your girl in a jiffy! Just slip the sundress on her, and tie the ribbons together at the shoulders. If the pillowcase you used was part of a set, you've got an extra to make another sundress…or check out the Easy, Breezy Skirt on page 124 to make something for yourself.

CHAPTER 3

Tools, Techniques, & Resources

The projects in this book range from advanced beginner to intermediate. Information about the tools and techniques required for these projects is given here.

TOOLS

I sewed every project in this book with a sewing machine, but many of them can also be sewn by hand, if preferred. For all of the projects, you'll need the basic set of tools listed at left. Additional tools are given in the Materials list at the start of each set of instructions.

WORKING WITH *SEWING GREEN* PATTERNS

Patterns are provided for all of the projects in this book that require them. Most of the patterns are found with the project directions. A few large, full-scale patterns (for example, for the Wrap Skirt on page 80 and the Lounge Pants on page 28) are provided on a pullout sheet inside the book's back cover (to keep the original patterns intact, I recommend copying these patterns by putting white shelf paper on top of them and tracing them). In the case of the smaller patterns, you'll find a note on each pattern piece indicating whether the pattern is shown at actual size or needs to be enlarged on a photocopier by the percentage noted. The patterns at actual size can be traced from the page using tracing paper or photocopied, enabling you to preserve the original pattern. Note that all the patterns include seam allowances. The width of those seam allowances may vary but is always clearly indicated in the project instructions.

BASIC TOOL LIST

Sewing machine

Universal needle

All-purpose sewing thread

Iron and ironing board

Press cloth

Seam ripper

Measuring tape or ruler

Straight pins

To cut out the patterns, either lay out the fabric flat and single-layer or fold the fabric in half, so you can cut two pieces at once. The pattern directions will tell you which way to lay out the fabric for cutting. To keep the patterns in place while cutting them out, I like to pin them to the fabric, placing the pins perpendicular to the pattern edges. I use fabric shears to cut out the pinned patterns and only recommend using a rotary cutter when a project has no pattern but gives measurements that require straight cuts, for example, an 8" square.

MACHINE STITCHES USED IN
SEWING GREEN

Backstitch: Also called back-tacking, backstitching is a simple way to anchor the stitches at the beginning and end of a seam. To backstitch at the start of a seam, position the needle a couple stitches ahead of where you want the seam to begin; push the machine's reverse button; stitch back to where the seam should begin; release the reverse button; and stitch forward, sewing over the several stitches you took in reverse. To backstitch at the end of a seam, push the reverse button, and stitch back several stitches over the forward stitches you just took. Note that backstitching by machine is very different from backstitching by hand (see page 134).

Edge-stitch: Edge-stitching involves sewing a row of stitches ⅛" or less from a folded or finished edge or from a seam line. Edge-stitching is generally visible on the right side of the finished work.

Machine-gather: To gather fabric by machine, lengthen your machine stitch to its longest setting, and slightly loosen the tension on the upper thread (the thread going through the needle; see your machine manual if you're unsure of how to adjust your machine's upper tension). Sew two parallel rows of stitches about ⅛" to ¼" away from the fabric's edge and ⅛" to ¼" apart from one another. Leave thread tails a couple inches long on each end of the stitched rows. Knot together the bottom (bobbin) threads on the two rows of stitches at one end of the area to be gathered. Gently pull the other end of the two bobbin threads, carefully sliding the fabric along the threads toward your knot and forming small gathers. After gathering your fabric to the needed length, securely knot the bobbin threads on the other end of the gathering rows with each other. Evenly distribute the gathering by gently sliding the "bunched" areas along the parallel threads. Then follow the project directions for permanently sewing the gathered edge.

Topstitch: Topstitching involves sewing a row of stitches more than ⅛" from a folded or finished edge or from a seam line. Topstitching, which is visible on the right side of the finished product, can be functional (that is, for example, it can anchor or help secure an edge) or purely decorative.

HANDSTITCHES

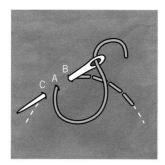

Backstitch

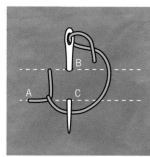

Blanket stitch

French knot

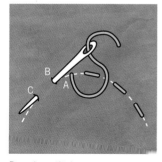

Running stitch

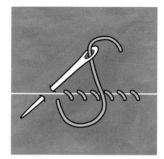

Whipstitch

HAND STITCHES USED IN *SEWING GREEN*

Backstitch: A backstitch is a strong stitch often used to anchor the beginning and end of a seam or a stitching line and can also be used to substitute hand-stitching for machine-stitching. However, backstitches can also be used decoratively, as they are in the Water-Bottle Sling on page 104. (Note that backstitching by hand is very different from backstitching by machine, described on page 133.)

To sew a backstitch by hand, work the stitch from right to left (or from left to right if you're left-handed): Bring the needle up from the wrong side of the fabric on the stitching line at A (see the drawing at left), insert it a short distance behind A at B, bring the needle back up in front of A at C, and pull the thread through. Insert the needle again just in front of A, and repeat the process, coming out a stitch length ahead of C. Continue stitching in this fashion for as long as needed.

Basting stitch: Hand-basting is used to temporarily hold two pieces of fabric together, so you can make sure that the placement of the seam is correct before permanently sewing the fabrics together by machine. To hand-baste two fabrics, place the pair in the desired position, and pin their edges together. Bring a needle with a knotted thread up through the fabric at the beginning of the stitching line; then stitch back down through the fabric and up again at ¼" intervals, making a series of long (¼"), even, and consistently spaced running stitches (see page 135) along the seam line. Secure the hand-basting by taking two backstitches (see above) close together.

After you've made sure that the seam line is correct, machine-stitch the fabrics together permanently. Then carefully remove the hand-basting stitches by picking out the backstitches with the tip of a seam ripper and pulling the thread from the knotted end to remove the rest of it.

Blanket stitch: A blanket stitch is a decorative stitch that can be used along the edge of a fabric or an appliqué. To sew a blanket stitch, work it from left to right (or from right to left if you're left-handed) with the thread moving between two imaginary lines about ¼" apart (see the drawing at left). Bring the needle up at A, stitch back down at B, and come up again at C, making sure the thread is under the needle. Note that the needle is oriented toward the fabric's (or appliqué's) raw or finished edge as you stitch. Pull on the thread to snug up the stitch, carefully aligning the thread loops along the edge of the fabric or appliqué, and continue stitching in this pattern across the entire edge.

French knot: This decorative stitch is easy to make: Bring the threaded needle up from the fabric's wrong side at A (see the drawing at left). Working close to the fabric, wrap the thread around the needle three times. Holding the thread wraps in place near the needle's point, insert the needle back into the fabric close to, but not in, A (if you stitch back into A, you'll lose the knot and have to begin again). Then pull the needle and thread out on the fabric's wrong side. Secure the thread on the back of the fabric if you're making just one French knot, or bring the needle back up to the front of the fabric at the position of the next knot. If you want to make a larger French knot, make more thread wraps around the needle.

Running stitch: This basic stitch is made by sewing from right to left (or from left to right if you're left-handed). To sew a running stitch, bring a threaded needle up from the wrong side of the fabric at A, stitch back down at B, and then come up again at C (see the drawing at left).Take stitches that are consistently about ⅛" long, and make the space between the stitches the same length as the stitches themselves. A basting stitch (see above) is simply a long (usually ¼" or more) running stitch.

Whipstitch: A whipstitch is an overhand stitch generally used to join two finished edges. To whipstitch, bring the needle up from the wrong side of the fabric though one of the edges being joined. Insert the needle down in the second edge, and bring it up again from the wrong side in the first edge. Continue inserting the needle from the fabric's back to front, taking small stitches and moving from right to left (or from left to right if you're left-handed) to join the two edges (see the drawing at left).

ONE-STEP BINDING WITH DOUBLE-FOLD BIAS TAPE AND MITERING A CORNER

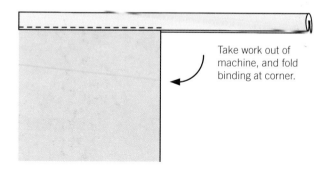

Stitch binding to one edge, stopping at corner.

Take work out of machine, and fold binding at corner.

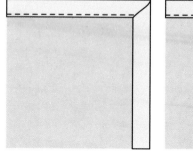

Make a diagonal pleat at corner and enclose perpendicular edge.

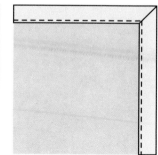

Stitch edge of binding, starting at pleat.

TERMS AND TECHNIQUES

Bias-Tape Binding: Bias tape is made from a strip of fabric cut on the fabric's bias, that is, at a 45-degree angle to the fabric's straight grain (see Grain Line on page 139). Bias tape is sold in varying widths and colors, usually in packages and prefolded in one of two ways, either single-fold and double-fold. Single-fold bias tape has a single fold running along each long edge of the tape. Double-fold bias tape likewise has a fold running along each edge of the tape, but it also has a center fold positioned slightly off-center, which results in having one of the long folded edges narrower than the other.

In the projects in this book, double-fold bias tape is used to bind a raw edge. The binding process can be done in one of two ways, one-step or two-step binding.

One-Step Binding: (This technique is used for the Vintage Napkins on page 24.) To bind an edge in a single step, begin with the project right side up. With the tape's narrow edge facing up, open the center fold of the bias with your fingers. Insert the edge of the fabric to be bound, right side up, in the fold of the tape so that it is sandwiched between the tape's layers and pin the tape in place to secure it. Stitch the binding as close as possible to the edge of the bias tape's narrow side, through all layers.

To bind a corner, sew the bias tape as described above to the corner of the fabric, remove the work from the machine, and clip the threads but do not cut the bias tape. Fold and pin the bias tape at the corner to form a neatly mitered pleat both on the top and bottom at the corner (see the drawings above), and also begin pinning the binding around the edge of the next side. Carefully place the mitered and pinned corner back under the machine's pressure foot, lower the needle into the edge of the mitered-corner pleat, backstitch (see page 133) a couple stitches at the mitered pleat to secure it, and then sew across the mitered pleat and down the binding to the next side.

TWO-STEP BINDING WITH DOUBLE-FOLD BIAS TAPE

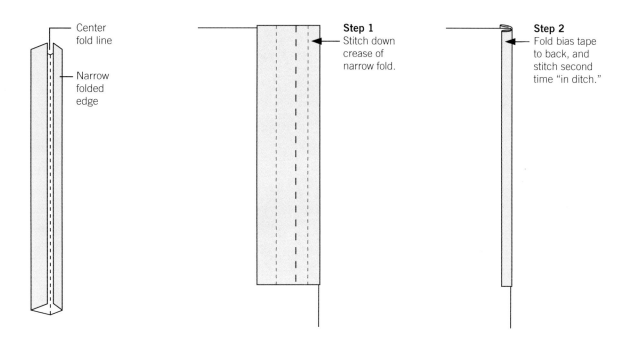

Center fold line

Narrow folded edge

Step 1
Stitch down crease of narrow fold.

Step 2
Fold bias tape to back, and stitch second time "in ditch."

Two-Step Binding: (This technique is used for the Auto Sunshade on page 110, Lunch Tote on page 86, and Girl's Easy, Breezy Sundress on page 128.)

1. Unfold the bias tape, and, with right sides together, align and pin the tape's narrow edge with the edge of the fabric being bound. Stitch along the crease of the tape's narrow fold, removing the pins as you sew (see the drawing above).

2. Fold and pin the bias tape to the back of the work, encasing the fabric's raw edges. Working from the wrong side, stitch along the length of the tape close to the folded edge; or, sewing from the right side, "stitch-in-the-ditch" (that is, topstitch directly into the "ditch" of the seam—the place where the two seamed fabrics meet—that you sewed in Step 1).

Note: It can be challenging to keep your topstitching straight when you're sewing through many layers, which is especially important if the stitches will appear in a noticeable place. Take the time to match your thread color to your fabric or bias tape, which will help your stitches blend in. Always practice new techniques on scraps before sewing on the real thing, stitching slowly and carefully. But most of all, relax— handmade items shouldn't have a mass-produced appearance. (Mine don't!)

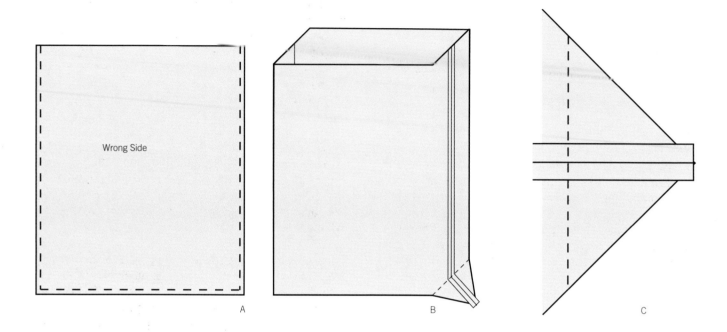

A   B   C

Boxing a corner: Adding box corners to the bottom of a bag gives it dimension and depth. To make a box corner, turn the bag wrong side out (see A), and align one side seam on top of the bag's bottom seam, creating a point at the corner (B), and pin in place. Measure 1½" (or the measurement given in the project instructions) from the corner point, mark a line perpendicular to the side seam. Sew on the marked line, backstitching (see page 133) at the beginning and end of the seam (C). Note that your seam line produces a triangle, which you should trim off after stitching. Repeat the process for the second corner.

Felting a sweater (or woven wool fabric): *Note: The process of felting knitted or woven wool is technically called "fulling"; however, the crafting community generally refers to it as felting. And, although the discussion below deals primarily with felting sweaters, the general directions also apply to wool garments.*

For optimal felting, check the content label of the sweater (or other garment) you plan to felt to make sure that it contains at least 90% wool (or a combination of wool and other animal fibers since synthetic fibers will not felt). If the sweater's care instructions suggest hand-washing or dry-cleaning only, chances are that it will felt well.

Using fabric shears, cut around the sweaters' armholes to remove the sleeves. Open up the sleeves by cutting the underarm seam. Then cut along the sweater body's side and shoulder seams to separate the front from the back.

Machine-wash the sweater pieces with detergent in hot water (washing similar colors together). After one wash cycle, check the progress of felting: The pieces should have shrunk, and the fabric should be thicker. If you can still see the individual stitches in the fabric or if it looks relatively unchanged, run the pieces through a second hot-wash cycle. When the felting has reached the desired result, dry the fabric in the dryer on a low setting. If the pieces come out of the dryer wrinkled, press them on the wrong side with a press cloth and a steam iron using the wool setting.

Fusible webbing: Double-sided fusible webbing is an iron-on adhesive used to bond fabric appliqués to a background fabric. There are several types of fusible webbing on the market. I suggest using a medium-weight webbing with a translucent paper backing on both sides. Working with double-sided webbing to bond an appliqué involves three steps:

1. Using paper scissors, cut out a piece of webbing slightly bigger than the size of the appliqué motif provided in the book. Place the webbing over the appliqué pattern, and use a pencil to trace the pattern onto the translucent paper on one side of the webbing. Peel the paper backing away from the other side of the webbing (not the paper side you drew on.)

2. Place the traced motif, with the paperless webbing side facing down on the wrong side of the fabric you're going to fuse. Following the manufacturer's directions, fuse the webbing to the fabric by ironing on the paper side, using a press cloth and a hot iron.

3. Using sharp scissors, cut out the fabric appliqué following the traced outline of the image. Remove the remaining paper from appliqué shape. Place the appliqué, webbing side down, on the fabric to which you want to fuse the appliqué. Cover the work with a press cloth, and fuse the appliqué with an iron to the background fabric

Grain line: The term *grain line* refers to the direction of the threads in a woven or knit fabric. A woven fabric is generally made up of a set of lengthwise threads (called warp threads) woven with a set of cross-wise threads (called weft threads). A woven fabric's *lengthwise grain* runs in the direction of the warp threads and is parallel to the fabric's selvedges (the tightly woven edges of the fabric). The fabric's *crosswise grain* runs in the direction of the weft threads, at a right angle to the lengthwise grain and the selvedges. The fabric's *bias* runs at a 45-degree angle to the lengthwise grain.

A knit fabric is generally made with a strand of yarn that is continuously looped, just like in hand-knitting, and the fabric's grain line usually runs vertically from the fabric's top to bottom (if you look closely at the knitted fabric, you'll see the straight vertical columns of stitches that make up the fabric's grain line).

Regardless of whether you're working with a woven or knit fabric, most patterns are intended to be aligned for cutting with the fabric's straight grain line. The patterns in this book carry a grain line arrow that should be aligned with the fabric's selvedge or its cut straight grain when positioning the pattern on the fabric. The pattern and project directions will specify if another layout for the pattern is required.

Lapped seam: To sew a lapped seam, position the two edges of the fabric you want to join with both fabrics right side up and with the top fabric's edge overlapping the bottom fabric's edge by about ½". Straight-stitch the overlapped edges ¼" from the edge of the top fabric, catching the fabric beneath it as well.

CLIPPING AND NOTCHING SEAM ALLOWANCES

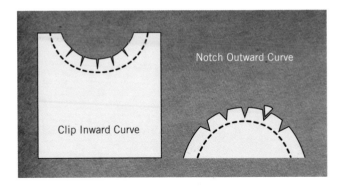

Pivoting: When machine-stitching a seam that has a corner or otherwise changes direction, you'll need to pivot the fabric to stitch in the new direction. To pivot, sew to the point where the stitching line changes direction, then stop with the needle down in the work. Next lift the presser foot, and rotate, or pivot, the work around the needle to reposition it. Lower the presser foot, and continue sewing in the new direction.

Seam allowance: The term *seam allowance* refers to the fabric between the stitched seam line and the fabric's raw, cut edge. A ¼" seam has seam allowances that are ¼" wide; a ½" seam has ½" seam allowances; and so on. If your seam is curved, the seam allowances may need to be clipped or notched (see below). Sometimes project directions will call for pressing the seam allowances open or to one side (see below).

Seam allowances, clipping or notching: Curved seam allowances need to be clipped (on inward curves) or notched (on outward curves) to allow the seam to lie flat and unpuckered when the sewn work is turned right side out. To clip a seam allowance, use fabric scissors to make small snips into the seam allowance perpendicular to the stitching line, being careful not to clip into the stitches themselves (see the drawing above). To notch a seam allowance, make angled clips into the allowance to remove small wedges of fabric.

Seam allowances, pressing: Project directions may tell you to press seam allowances open or to one side. To press seam allowances open, lay the project wrong side up on the ironing board. Separate the two seam allowances with your fingers, then carefully press them open flat with the iron.

To press seam allowances to one side, again lay the work wrong side up on the ironing board, then press both seam allowances together to one side of the seam line (the project directions will usually tell you which side to press them to; if they don't, you can press them to either side). If the project directions don't mention pressing the seam allowances, you can leave them unpressed.

RESOURCES

Most of the materials and tools used in the projects in this book—with the exception of the recycled materials and possibly some of the organic materials and specialty items listed below—are available at fabric stores nationwide. If you cannot find what you are looking for locally, try these online sources:

www.fabric.com
www.joann.com
www.mjtrim.com
www.purlsoho.com
www.reprodepot.com
www.sewmamasew.com

ORGANIC & ECO-FRIENDLY FABRICS/MATERIALS

Nature-Fil bamboo fiber
(used for Baby Toy, page 74)

Fairfield Processing
PO Box 1130
Danbury, CT 06813
(800) 980-8000
www.poly-fil.com/naturefil.asp

Print organic cotton sateen
(used for Lunch Tote, page 86)

Harmony Art
PO Box 892
Gualala, CA 95445
(707) 884-3347
www.harmonyart.com

Organic cotton herringbone check
(used for Baby Quilt, page 70);
Organic terry and organic gingham
(used for Washies, page 70)

Michael Miller Fabrics, LLC
118 West 22nd Street, 5th Floor
New York, NY 10011
(212) 704-0774
www.michaelmillerfabrics.com

Eco Craft pillow forms
(used for Graphic Pillows, page 40)

Mountain Mist
2551 Crescentville Road
Cincinnati, OH 45241
(800) 345-7150
www.mountainmistlp.com

Heirloom cotton batting and organic cotton sherpa
(used for Baby Quilt, page 70)
Natural cotton leno
(used for Natural Produce Bags, page 100)

NearSea Naturals, Incorporated
PO Box 345
Rowe, NM 87562
(877) 573-2913
www.nearseanaturals.com

Natural terry velour
(used for Cashmere Throw, page 134, and Heat Therapy Pillow, page 66)

Organic Cotton Plus
822 Baldridge Street
O'Donnell, TX 79351
(806) 428-3345
www.organiccottonplus.com

Although I didn't use fabrics from the companies listed below, their fabrics are sustainable, innovative, beautiful, and definitely worth checking out.

Mod Green Pod
www.modgreenpod.com
Printed organic home-decorating fabrics

Oliveira Textiles
www.oliveiratextiles.com
Sustainable home-decorating textiles

The Cork Store
www.corkstore.com
Fabrics and other products made from natural cork

greenSTYLE by Robert Kaufman Fabrics
www.robertkaufman.com/green
Organic, sustainable and eco-friendly fabrics

SPECIALTY ITEMS

Microwavable whole buckwheat seeds
(used in the Heat-Therapy Pillow, page 66)

Buckwheat can be purchased in bulk at health food stores or at various online stores, including the following:
www.buckwheathull.com
www.nutsonline.com

Nikwax waterproofing products
(used on the Beach Tote, page 120)

Nikwax is a nontoxic product designed to make fabrics waterproof, and is especially useful for preventing stains on light-colored fabrics. Nikwax products can be purchased at outdoor apparel retailers, such as www.rei.com. For more information, visit www.nikwax.com

PUL (Polyurethane Laminate)
(PUL fabric with laminated back used for the Sandwich Wrap, page 90; PUL fabric with laminated front used for the lining of the Lunch Tote, page 86)

PUL refers to any fabric that has been laminated with polyurethane on one side to make it waterproof. These fabrics are often found online on websites that sell fabric cuts for making diaper covers as well as at some larger chain fabric stores.

www.celticclothswholesale.com
www.diapercuts.com
www.knickernappies.com
www.mimithesardine.com

RECYCLED/REPURPOSED MATERIALS

To locate thrift stores in your area, visit the following websites or check your local telephone directory:

Nationwide Directories
www.thethriftshopper.com
www.thriftyplanet.com

Goodwill Industries
http://locator.goodwill.org
www.shopgoodwill.com (to buy online!)

The Salvation Army Stores
www.satruck.com/findstore.asp
To find secondhand items from individuals in your community, try these online resources:

www.craigslist.org
www.freecycle.org

WEBSITES AND BLOGS

Here is a list of a few of the many eco-oriented websites that I like to visit.

Crafting a Green World
www.craftingagreenworld.com
A blog featuring do-it-yourself projects that incorporate reused, recycled, and natural materials.

Eco Chick
www.eco-chick.com
Rather than catering to guys or moms, this eco-blog is for the hip green chicks.

Enviromom
www.enviromom.com
A blog for moms that subscribe to the "baby step" approach to making lifestyle changes.

Green Home Guide
www.greenhomeguide.com
Simple, helpful green tips for the home.

Ideal Bite
www.idealbite.com
Easy eco-living tips delivered daily in a short, sassy email.

The International Oeko-Tex Association
www.oekotex.com
This association created the Oeko-Tex Standard 100, an independent test that checks textiles for harmful substances. The Oeko-Tex Standard 100 is used globally to certify textiles at all stages of production, and has textile research and test institutes in over 40 countries worldwide.

International Working Group on Global Organic Textile Standard
www.global-standard.org
An organization that has developed a set of standards that are accepted worldwide which ensure the organic status of textiles and provide a credible assurance to the consumer. Standards apply to all levels of cultivation and production, from harvesting of raw materials, to environmentally and socially responsible manufacturing, to labeling of products.

The Lazy Environmentalist
www.lazyenvironmentalist.com
Easy, stylish, and super convenient ways to green your lifestyle with Josh Dorfman, author of *The Lazy Environmentalist*.

Mindful Momma
www.mindfulmomma.typepad.com
A family-oriented blog with lively conversation on being mindful, finding balance, and enjoying what we have.

The Organic Trade Association
www.ota.com
OTA is a business association for the organic industry. Straight facts about what it takes to be organic.

Sew Green
www.sewgreen.blogspot.com
A collaborative blog covering everyday green topics and crafting.

Simply Green
www.dannyseo.typepad.com
Blog by green-living expert Danny Seo.

Treehugger
www.treehugger.com
Dedicated to making sustainability mainstream, this is a one-stop shop for green news, solutions, and product information.

Wardrobe Refashion
www.nikkishell.typepad.com/wardroberefashion
Take a 2- to 4-month pledge to abstain from new clothing purchases while creating a wardrobe from on-hand, repurposed materials.

WorldChanging
www.worldchanging.com
Worldchanging is a solutions-based online magazine focused on building a better future.

The Worsted Witch
www.worstedwitch.com
Crafting mixed with great information about sustainability.

NOTEWORTHY MAGAZINES

These are four of the eco-oriented magazines I read.

ReadyMade
www.readymade.com

CRAFT
craftzine.com/magazine

Natural Home
www.naturalhomemagazine.com

The Green Guide
www.thegreenguide.com

ACKNOWLEDGMENTS

I am forever grateful to the following people who contributed their time and talents to *Sewing Green*.

To my editor, Melanie Falick, for her direction and dedication to the vision of this book.

To my agents, Lilly Ghahremani and Stefanie Von Borstel, for their steadfast support and expertise.

To Liana Allday, for her guidance and sunny disposition.

To Chris Timmons and Betty Christiansen, for gently nudging my words into something clear and refined.

To Raina Kattelson, John Gruen, and Sarah Von Dreele for making everything look so beautiful.

To my niece, Alice Wetterlund, for gracing the cover of this book with her beauty.

To the lovely models, Liana Allday, Bella and Lorna Brundrett, Maeve and Romi Butscher, Stella Cornelion, Alicia Davis, Sharon Maurer, Grace Nowakoski, Julia Spiegel, Ann Stratton, Dalia Strohmeidav, and Alice Wetterlund. Thank you for your time, patience, and charm.

To Altomari Sew/Vac Center (Kingston, NY), Jill Cornelion, Pat Garofal, and Hammertown Barn (Rhinebeck, NY), for supplying props and clothing for the photo shoot that added just the right touch.

To Martin Clarke, Fab Yarns (Tivoli, NY), George Smith, Julia Spiegel, and Gordon Ticehurst, for welcoming us into their homes and businesses for photography.

To Lisa DuWell, for her pattern-making expertise.

Special thanks to Natalie Chanin, Wendy Tremayne, Crispina ffrench, Claire Morsman, and Harmony Susalla, for taking time out of their busy schedules to share their knowledge and experiences with me.

It has been an honor to work with all of you.

To my family—my mom, Jan; my dad, Jack; my mother-in-law, Virginia; my brothers, Scott and Roger; my sisters-in-law Kris and Christy—thank you for your love, support, and ongoing encouragement. And a very special thank you to my husband, Dave, and my boys, Conner and Sean, for being inspirations in my life, for making me laugh, and for reminding me of what really matters in this world.

 In loving memory of my grandmother, Frances T. Sayre, a woman whose style, practicality, and philosophy of "waste not, want not" stay with me today.

Published in 2009 by Stewart, Tabori & Chang
An imprint of Harry N. Abrams, Inc.

Text copyright © 2009 by Betz White
All photographs except on pages 32 and 38 copyright © 2009 by John Gruen
Photographs on page 32 © Luiza Leite and SORR
Photograph on page 38 © Robert Rausch

Library of Congress Cataloging-in-Publication Data:
White, Betz.
Sewing green : 25 Projects Made with Repurposed
& Organic Materials, Plus Tips & Resources for Earth-Friendly
Stitching/by Betz White.
p. cm.
ISBN 978-1-58479-758-6

1. Clothing and dress--Remaking. 2. Recycling (Waste, etc.) I. Title.

TT550.W54 2009
646.4--dc22
2008023649

Editors: Melanie Falick and Liana Allday
Technical Editor: Christine Timmons
Designer: Onethread
Production Manager: Jacqueline Poirier

The text of this book was composed in Clarendon, Trade Gothic, and Coquette.

Printed and bound in China.
10 9 8 7 6 5 4 3 2 1

harry n. abrams, inc.
a subsidiary of La Martinière Groupe

115 West 18th Street
New York, NY 10011
www.hnabooks.com